Praise for *Not Ju...*

"I cannot say enough about this book! I only wish I had this book earlier. Through sharing her own family's inspiring story, Ms. Laird offers much needed education and support for parents and grandparents of children with SPD. Ms. Laird has a special insight into this confusing and often misunderstood disorder. Even though my daughter and I live with this every day, I learned a lot from this book, and will return to my family with renewed hope and energy!"
—Nancy Pfortmiller

"*Not Just Spirited* is a deep from the gut and heart story of life with her daughter who was diagnosed (finally) with a sensory processing disorder. It ain't pretty, but it is compelling. Reading that her pediatrician insisted on repeatedly dismissing the mounting evidence as a "just spirited" child is a familiar story to many but no less galling. It is even worse when a parent is tied to the physician for the sake of required referrals. Living with a severely atypical child can be hell. As Laird clearly points out, no one who hasn't lived with such a child can appreciate the difficulty. That difficulty doesn't even take into account the corrosion it visits on a marriage. Congratulations to Laird for helping to empower parents."
—Andrew D. Gibson, PhD
author *Got an Angry Kid? Parenting Spike, a Seriously Difficult Child*

"Not Just Spirited is at once an excellent—and possibly unique —introduction to this disorder; a field guide; a treatment manual; a pep talk; and a compendium of the state of the art in coping techniques, tips, and advice. This is the story of one family, one mother who would not give up on her daughter. It is also an indictment of clinical psychology at the outset of the new millennium: a profession gone ossified and resistant to evidence and new learning, rendering more harm than good whenever confronted with the unknown."
—Sam Vaknin, PhD
author of *Malignant Self-love: Narcissism Revisited*"

"The story of the relentless power of a parent's love, this book chronicles the first five years of learning to live with Sensory Processing Disorder. Accurate diagnosis and partnership with kind, adaptive teachers take the author from heartbreak to hope. I also came away from this book with awe for the power of how innately adept children are at teaching each other."

—Nancy Oelklaus, EdD
author, *Journey From Head to Heart*

not JUSt spirited

A Mom's Sensational Journey With Sensory Processing Disorder (SPD)

Chynna T. Laird

Foreword by Dr. Shane Steadman

Loving Healing Press

2nd Printing: January 2010

Library of Congress Cataloging-in-Publication Data
Laird, Chynna T., 1970-
  Not just spirited : a mom's sensational journey with sensory processing disorder (SPD) / Chynna T. Laird.
     p. cm.
  Includes bibliographical references and index.
  ISBN-13: 978-1-61599-008-5 (trade paper : alk. paper)
  ISBN-10: 1-61599-008-9 (trade paper : alk. paper)
  1. Sensory integration dysfunction in children--Popular works.
I. Title.
  RJ496.S44L35 2010
  618.92'8--dc22
                                        2009035454

Published by
Loving Healing Press
5145 Pontiac Trail
Ann Arbor, MI 48105

Distributed by Ingram Book Group (USA/CAN), Bertrams Books (UK), Hachette Group (EU), New Leaf Distributing (USA/CAN)

www.LovingHealing.com
info@LovingHealing.com
phone 888-761-6268

Contents

Foreword i

Acknowledgements i

Introduction – Good Things Happen To Those Who Wait v
    What is SPD? vii
    What are the Sensory Systems Affected by SPD?................................. viii
    What Causes SPD?... x
    Is SPD a "Real" Diagnosis? xi
    Sharing Our Stories.. xii

Chapter 1 – I Saw the Sign 1

Chapter 2 – "Just Spirited" Are You Kidding Me?............................... 11

Chapter 3 – Steve's Story: "Daddy Loves You"................................... 19

Chapter 4 – …And Baby Makes Four: The Confirmation 25

Chapter 5 – The Last Straw 33

Chapter 6 – One Step Forward, Two Steps Back… 47

Chapter 7 – Chynna's Story: "Loving with a Musical Touch" 59

Chapter 8 – The Long and Winding Road of Therapy 63

Chapter 9 – HELP!... 79

Chapter 10 – Babies, Brain Food, Jenna, and Fun Factory: Our Holistic Approach 91

Chapter 11 – Teaching Teachers, and Other Grown-Ups, How To Teach 113

Chapter 12 – Blackbird Fly: Endnotes for Parents 127

About the Author: Chynna T. Laird 139

Resources and Websites 141

Bibliography... 143

Index.. 147

Foreword

Many parents come into my office frustrated, confused, and overwhelmed with the behavior or disposition their children. They often relate that teachers, counselors, friends, and family are constantly commenting that their child is disruptive, distracted, daydreaming, or cannot focus. They have been all over from practitioner to practitioner getting a label (sometimes different ones) and some treatment, but no real fix to their problems. Eventually, I hear how frustrated they are and how much money has been spent with little results or answers.

When going through the child's health history, often the parents will mention that there has always been something different about their kid. Sometimes they will tell me that their child was so advanced because he or she was extremely alert—never crawled, and just went straight to walking. They will often describe them as picky eaters, highly sensitive to their environment, or irritable. As their child has grown and developed, they have seen things that were not like other children such as being by themselves, not wanting to be touched, not walking barefoot, a daredevil, hyperactive, or not wanting to wear clothes. As you read this paragraph one might think, "He or she will grow out of it," while others would think, "There must be something wrong with that kid." Well, which one is it? This becomes the daily struggle of many parents as they become frustrated and overwhelmed looking for answers.

Sensory Processing Disorder (SPD) is becoming more prevalent as time goes on. It also appears that more attention is given to these cases and therapies are being established to help those kids function in society. There are many factors involved in SPD as well as many symptoms associated with this diagnosis. Some of the symptoms include hypersensitivity to touch, sensitivity to sound, and exhibiting distress, or confusion. Many factors range from prenatal care, genetic predispositions, and lifestyle to post-natal care and traumas. Often SPD becomes confused or misdiagnosed with other types of labels such as Attention Deficit Disorder (ADD), Autism Spectrum Disorder (ASD) or just labeled as gifted. Finally, there can be other conditions to address (known as co-morbidity) such as Tourette's, dyslexia, and OCD.

After conversations with Chynna and reading her book, I can tell you her story is just one example of what many parents are going through. Chynna shares her experience as a mother of a child with SPD. Her story is one of frustration, confusion, and fear only to leave the reader with sense of hope and relief at the end. Unfortunately, there are many parents that feel alone in the process of doctor appointments after doctor appointments, therapies after therapies, comments after comments all leading to a feeling a frustration, fear, isolation, and confusion. Hopefully reading Chynna and Steve's story will give any caregiver a sense of hope and relief at the end of their story.

As I'm writing this Foreword, I'm also watching my son Zach yell, make noises, and trying to figure out how to put toys into his mouth. Just three weeks ago, we went through a similar frustration as our family friends would comment on his behavior. They would mention that he seemed unresponsive and delayed. Just to get a second opinion, we went and saw a pediatrician who referred us to a pediatric neurologist. By the end of those two visits, we were told that a MRI was going to be done to rule out a tumor or a stroke as they were not sure what it was. Even though I see kids in my office regularly with developmental problems it makes it hard to turn the "Dad" button off. We found ourselves riding a rollercoaster of emotions and frustrated with the process. All tests came back normal but they gave me a small glimpse of what some parents go through on a daily basis.

Sensory Processing Disorder is a diagnosis that is becoming more understood. There are therapies designed to help those with

SPD ranging from Occupational Therapies to Complimentary and Alternative Therapies. What is exciting to me is how well the brain can learn new things, improve, and increase its function. Chynna's book is a great tool for many struggling parents trying to figure out where to start. This book is easy to read and informative as it will draw you into the emotions of their journey. A great message for the newly diagnosed or even the experienced person.

Dr. Shane Steadman, D.C., D.A.C.N.B., C.C.C.N., C.N.S.
Board Certified Chiropractic Neurologist
Certified Nutrition Specialist

Acknowledgements

This book started off as journal entries—a way for me to make sense of what was happening to my daughter as well as being a positive emotional release for me. From there I was inspired to help make sure no parents I came in contact with would go through as much heartache as we did. I have several people I've met along my journey to thank for helping me bring this story out giving me the strength to share it. My support group is small but each of them has had a special part in helping me get to where I am:

Thank you to Steve for his patience and support. He never once complained having to care for our four little beauties so I had writing time or for having to stare at the back of my head while I wrote, edited and re-edited.

Thank you to my fabulous little PR group: Judy, who has been like a mother to me the last 10 years; Uncle Craig and Aunt Dorothy, who have always been there for me through thick and thin, good and bad, elation and pain and never let me believe the words, "I can't,"; Grandpa and Grandma for giving me the regular love, parenting and stability I needed as a child to believe in myself and not become a statistic (I know you're both watching over me...I love you and miss you); Angela, Jodi, Annette, Margo, Ruth, Allyn, Krysten and all my other gal-writing-pals at WOW-womenonwriting, without you, I'd never have had the courage to pick up the ball and keep writing; and Carole Bellacera, Mary Rosenblum, and Francie, you are my writing mentors and inspire me each day to keep writing.

Thank you to the phenomenal people in the SPD Community from whom I've learned so much about SPD, mothering, and life: Dr. A. Jean Ayres, Carol Stock Kranowitz, Dr. Lucy Jane Miller, Winnie Dunn, and all the other influential people who've done/are doing powerful SPD research and are continuing to teach Dr. Ayres' message; Carrie Finnin, Erik and Jennie Linthorst, Diane Renna, Bonnie Arnwine, Lisa Rudley, Hartley Steiner and all sensational parents out there doing sensational things to give other parents inspiration and hope.

Thank you so much to those whose eyes saw what I didn't and helped steer me on the right path: Donna Gravelle, the first person who worked with Jaimie and guided us down the first baby steps; Joan McDonald, who shared her personal story with her own daughter with me and gave me valuable insight I needed; Brian Lotannas, who gave Steve the tools to connect with his daughter; Lori Fankhanel words cannot express the gratitude I have for your friendship, guidance and pearls of wisdom; and Kathy Mulka, who opened my eyes wider to Jaimie's needs and helped me see what I'd missed—you are an angel on earth. I'm also so grateful to Mary Turos for her invaluable insight on helping people understand the connection among the brain and learning and for teaching the world the importance of teaching each child according to their own unique style of learning not how the systems states kids *should be* learning. To Mrs. P., Kathy Young, Ms. Eisan and the other phenomenal people at Sweet Grass Elementary—thanks for making my child feel accepted, loved and save at school.

Thank you to Jenna, Rita, Maddie, Meka, Chloe and the rest of Jaimie's friends who've never once treated Jaimie as "different" and for accepting her for who she is. Know that no matter whether she's out there smiling and playing with you or lost inside of herself your friendship is always treasured.

Thank you to Victor R. Volkman and the fabulous people at Loving Healing Press that fussed over and tweaked our story so that it all makes sense. I appreciate all of your support and hard work. Also, special thanks to Ernest Dempsey and Laurie Zelinger, PhD who helped proof and edit the many drafts.

Finally, and most importantly, thank you to my baby girl, Jaimie. You are my miracle girl and a true gift from God. You've taught me patience, love, understanding, respect and to see people for more than what is on the outside. You've taught me that failure isn't an option because as long as you try, it counts. And you've shown me the world from a very different perspective— I'm so grateful. You are the bravest little person I know and you'll go far, I'm sure. Mama loves you.

Introduction – Good Things Happen To Those Who Wait

It was a task I'd done a million times—something as simple as changing my 15-month-old daughter, Jaimie's, diaper. But her reaction to such a mundane chore sent a chill through my bones.

"No!" Jaimie screamed as I laid her back on the change table.

"Be still, sweetie. This'll only take a minute."

Instead of calming her, my voice seemed to upset her more. She covered her ears with her hands, screwed her eyes shut, and banged her head against the table. "No, no, noooooooooooooooo!" she screeched, the dull thud of her head against the wood emphasizing every 'no'.

Only when her feet touched the ground again did her hands come off her ears and her screaming cease. I watched her run from the room, leaving me with ringing in my ears and heaviness in my heart. Fighting back tears of frustration, I knew something was very wrong. This just wasn't normal.

From an outsider's perspective, this would seem somewhat normal behavior for a toddler. However, Jaimie's behavior wasn't stemming from not getting her way. As we found out later on, she was unable to cope in the world around her and wasn't able to communicate this to me in any other way. Adding to her frustration was her total dislike of being held, comforted, or otherwise touched. Jaimie was basically trapped in a struggle between wanting to be comforted and touched but her body being utterly repulsed by the feeling of touch. Everyone thought I was nuts, but just *knew* something was wrong with Jaimie as early as three months into her life.

While other wee ones seemed comforted with touching, hugs, and kisses, Jaimie was the opposite. Whenever we picked her up, she struggled and screamed but calmed down, somewhat, as soon as we put her back down. As she grew, the small odd things I'd noticed about her temperament grew with her: she adjusted slowly to change, startled easily, rarely smiled or laughed, and was so afraid of other people that I spent entire visits or shopping trips with Jaimie clinging desperately to me. A simple, "Hi there!" from a stranger, or even her own Daddy, triggered tears immediately.

On top of this, Jaimie had terrible fits where she hurt herself in some way—such as head banging, biting herself or other people/objects, scratching herself, or pulling out her hair—on purpose.

Whenever I addressed my concerns with family or friends, I was made to feel I was reading too much into things because I was a first time mom. Even Jaimie's pediatrician said her behavior was simply chalked up to "spiritedness" and we just needed to have patience with her.

"She'll grow out of this stage soon enough," he said at the end of each visit.

When Jaimie's behavior worsened to the point where she had fits for hours at a time every day, I knew she needed help far beyond what I could handle on my own. When she was about two and a half, Jaimie's pediatrician finally listened to my pleas and directed us to an Early Intervention Program. After only one visit, the occupational therapist (OT), named Donna, who specialized in children with sensory issues, was able to deduce Jaimie's behavior down to three words: Sensory Processing Disorder (SPD) [At the time, she'd called it Sensory Integration Dysfunction, or SID.]

While reading our story, it's important for people to remember that Jaimie's form of SPD is quite severe, with all her sensory systems being affected at some level. It's also important to remember that Jaimie's form of SPD isn't common. Most children who have SPD usually only have one or two systems affected and can still function relatively fine once they've learned to recognize their symptoms as well as learned positive coping skills.

This book is intended to be as jargon-free as possible because I felt parents and other people dealing with children who have SPD have heard, and will hear, enough of it during their own assessment, diagnosis, and treatment stages. For those readers who may be unfamiliar with SPD, I've included general information on the subject, descriptions of the specific systems affected by SPD as well as some believed causes.

What is SPD?

The simplest definition of SPD is, "The inability for the brain to process information received through the senses." (Kranowitz, 2005). The hardest part about SPD is giving it a solid definition. The main reason for this is that no two children experience the exact same symptoms or the same severity of symptoms. Children are categorized as either over-responsive or under-responsive to sensory stimulation. Their brains aren't giving their bodies the appropriate messages to understand how to interact properly with objects, people, and situations in their environment. This can cause them to either seek out or avoid sensory stimulation in ways that seem excessive or odd to us in order to "feel" it in a way that's comfortable to them.

An over-responsive child is one who freaks out with even the slightest sensory stimulation. For example, an odor that's barely detectable can cause him to gag; or a neon light will actually hurt his eyes; or he's easily startled by noise, no matter how loud or soft it may seem to others.

An under-responsive child is the opposite. These children don't seem to respond to stimulation at all. For example, there could be a lot of activity in a room but they don't acknowledge it; or the child will hit himself with something but not react. Sensory seekers, on the other hand, are children who need way more stimulation than the average child to "feel" something. For example, when my Jaimie was very stressed, she needed to have the television, stereo, her toys, and my computer on at the same time *and* still sought more noise in order to cope. Odd as it may seem, this calmed her.

Donna told me to keep in mind, however, that SPD children may not stay within one category. They may have symptoms spreading out within the three areas. With Jaimie, for example, were times where she needed the over-stimulation as described above but then there were times where even the noise of me pulling the tabs apart to change her diaper had her covering her ears and screaming, "It hurts!" (over-responsive). Finally, there were also times where we'd called her name repeatedly and she wouldn't respond until we stood right in front of her so she saw us (under-responsive). This uncertainty may not be reassuring but getting the diagnosis is the first step in giving parents a sense of direction in how they can help their child cope.

What are the Sensory Systems Affected by SPD?

The most commonly known sensory systems are the visual (vision), olfactory (smell), auditory (hearing) and, gustatory (taste). These systems work together with the following systems, called Primary Systems, to give us information about our environments and how to relate to the people and objects in our environments:

(1) **Tactile** – This is the sense of touch. In addition to feeling things—touching and being touched—this system also sends the brain messages about things like pressure on the skin, temperature, and the awareness of our bodies. Essentially, when

this system is out of whack, we don't feel safe in the world around us because we never know how something is going to feel.

Jaimie, for example, isn't able to handle even light touch. It drives her crazy. When she's very sensitive, she fights having a bath, getting her hair brushed or having her teeth brushed; she doesn't like the feel of her clothes; won't go outside if it's too windy, or even refuses to have anyone sit too close to her. To her, such things send a "pain" message to her brain and she goes into immediate sensory overload.

There are other times, however, where Jaimie can shove her hands into snow, hold ice cubes, hit parts of her body on other objects or touch something burning hot and she won't feel the sensation until much later on. This aspect of SPD, the under-responsive side, is scarier because children can seriously injure themselves if they aren't paying attention.

(2) **Vestibular** – This is one of the gravity senses that tells the brain about movement. This sense tells the body whether we're moving or not, what direction we're going in, and how fast. It works closely with the visual system to help develop good eye muscle control, eye perception, and attention span. The vestibular system is also in charge of our coordination, balance, muscle tone, and fine motor skills (hand control and dominance). As you can imagine, children with poor vestibular systems struggle with fine and gross motor skills and are often seen as clumsy or "ragdoll-like" (poor muscle tone and control.)

On bad days, Jaimie walks into things, trips, and falls down a lot; isn't able to concentrate on anything; and struggles with simple tasks like bouncing a ball, hopping on one foot or cutting paper with scissors.

(3) **Proprioceptive** – Essentially this is just a big word to say it's the system that tells us what our bodies are doing. It allows us to gauge, for example, how close we are to something or someone where our bodies are in the environment. The system takes infor-

mation from joints and muscles and helps us to learn skilled movements.

Children struggling in this area will have trouble coordinating their bodies to do activities like bouncing a ball, playing coordinating sports—like baseball or hockey—and are terrified of heights, being picked up or held upside down or activities like ice-skating where we can lose a sense of control over our bodies.

It's important to know about all of these sensory systems in order to understand why a child like Jaimie may react negatively to a certain activity, person, or experience. And one should also bear in mind that what may bother a child with SPD on one day may not even faze him, or her, the next. It's one of the most confusing and frustrating aspects of helping and raising a child with SPD.

What Causes SPD?

I asked Donna this very question because the books I'd read hadn't been very clear. Unfortunately, Donna's answer was no clearer: "There could be many explanations for it, from what I've learned," she said. "The truth is, nobody has been able to pin point this for certain. Currently, the most plausible explanations are genetic or hereditary predispositions, meaning it comes from one or the other parent, prenatal circumstances, or birth trauma. But these are only *possible* explanations and not definite."

Donna also mentioned that once some parents figure out what's wrong with their children, they've actually said they'd remembered experiencing similar feelings as children. So, perhaps, there *is* a genetic component causing the child to be predisposed to develop the disorder but an environmental factor must occur in order for it to come to the surface or become phenotypical.

Personally, I've stopped trying to find a solid explanation because I only end up pointing the finger at myself and this doesn't help Jaimie at all. If I've learned anything, it's not to waste time to find blame, but to use the time to find out what proactive things can be done to help Jaimie. Our child doesn't blame us so we shouldn't either.

Is SPD a "Real" Diagnosis?

Parents whose children receive a diagnosis of SPD may ask themselves this initially—Steve and I did. When Jaimie was diagnosed with SPD four years ago, I'd never heard of it. I'd heard of autism, Asperger's, and ADHD but not this mysterious SPD. In fact, I was taking a Brain and Behavior course through the University of British Columbia and my professor, Dr. John Pinel—who is a well-known and well-respected Canadian Neurologist—and, incidentally who wrote my text book for the course—hadn't heard of it either! In an email, he'd actually told me he had to "Google" SPD and visit my website to have any clue what I was asking him about. That both scared and angered me.

Although SPD was discovered in the late 1960s by A. Jean Ayres, and has been researched for over 35 years, there hasn't been enough massive, controlled "quantified" research to prove/disprove or predict symptoms or life course of the disorder. That's the pulse of research: to create a theory that continues by other researchers trying to prove/disprove it. Because of the difficulty—until recently—to have variables and controls to study, there aren't actual statistics to provide. Plus, because SPD has many symptoms that mirror other disorders (called "co-morbidity")—such as autism, Asperger's ADHD, to name only a few—it makes it even more difficult to create a solid controlled research environment.

According to the Sensory Processing Disorder website (www.sensory-processing-disorder.com), another reason for the difficulties with researching SPD is that a child's symptoms can fluctuate from one day, even one hour some days, to the next. This makes it very difficult to find a controlled environment to conduct studies and the fluctuations in symptoms also make it hard to find solid numbers to create statistics. Additionally, SPD is considered a relatively new diagnosis so there are many people who have it—even as adults—and don't even realize it. In fact, I am friends with a woman who always knew something was different about her but never knew why. She said her environment was a very uncomfortable and scary place for her at times growing up. Imagine her surprise to be diagnosed at age 35 with SPD! Then everything she'd gone through made sense to her.

One thing we've also had people say to us is that, "We all experience sensory overload at some point." This is true. But, as you'll see in our story, it becomes a problem, or a disorder, when that sensory overload happens frequently and impedes on a person's ability to live their lives productively.

So, to answer the question: Yes, SPD is a real disorder. The fact that the name has universally changed from "Sensory Integration Dysfunction" to "Sensory Processing Disorder" just in the last few years is a huge step. With support from leading researchers, such as Dr. Lucy Jane Miller, who carry on the work that Dr. A. Jean Ayres' work that she started so many years ago, SPD will finally be included in the next revision to the DSM as a neurological disorder. This means that families will qualify for insurance coverage for treatment of SPD and our children will finally have the additional support of the medical community.

Sharing Our Stories

How was I supposed to help my daughter, or even help others understand her, when nobody knew what this disorder was? Once I researched it, however, and created my website, I found many resources and websites to help educate myself. I knew I couldn't have been the only parent out there who not only didn't know about SPD but also didn't know anyone else going through it. That's when I started using my gift of writing to reach out to others and give them permission to reach out to me.

What I needed to ask myself was: Who the heck would be interested in reading our story? I got my answer after the first story I published on the subject of mothering a child with SPD. After the story came out, my email Inbox flooded with letters from other moms of SPD children, thanking me for sharing my story. It still amazes me how many of us are out there: parents who want their children to be happy in a world frightening them and causing them pain.

What we need is more research to find out for sure. With research, we can discover the root of the cause; then understand how to treat these children most effectively. But without acknowledgement and discussion, there won't be any research. And without research, there will be no understanding.

And that's why we need stories, like Jaimie's and those like her, told to help bring about awareness. There are so many wonderful resource tools out there written by occupational therapists, doctors, and other professionals. Here's a resource from a Mommy who simply wants people to see *her child* and not just her reactions to her surroundings. As I always say, "Through awareness comes understanding and that's so powerful."

Here's our story...

1 | I Saw the Sign

By the time Jaimie was about three months old, I'd already suspected she struggled with…something. Actually, I knew in the hospital after I gave birth to her but my suspicions were confirmed when she was about three months old.

I noticed that whenever the nurses in the hospital handled Jaimie, or even when they'd given her to me to feed, her tiny body stiffened and her cries worsened. But when she was put back down, she relaxed, and then seemed to calm enough to go to sleep. When I'd asked the nurses about Jaimie's odd reactions, they'd said it wasn't unusual for babies to fuss right after birth. After all, babies had to get used to life outside the womb.

"Don't worry so much," I was told. "You're a first-time Mom and it's natural to worry about every little thing. Relax and she will too."

Relax. Don't worry so much. I heard those words a lot over the next while. Yes, I was a first-time Mom and, perhaps, even a bit nervous. And I was the first to admit that I had a fierce protection of Jaimie because Steve and I had worked so hard to conceive her. But I knew when to worry and, from my experience with helping to care for children, knew the difference between a "fussy" baby and a "troubled" baby. Even the most colicky babies felt better being held or just being near you than when they'd be put down. Not Jaimie.

She startled easily, screamed when she was held or cuddled, and pulled her limbs closely to her body whenever anyone tried touching her. I'd never seen anything like that before. But after continuously being told by the nursing staff and doctors that it was just my first-time Mom jitters kicking in, I stopped addressing it. I'd decided everyone else must have been right— they were the experts, after all—if I was the only one seeing Jaimie's odd behavior. I figured Jaimie would work it out on her own and that she just needed to get used to us, her environment and all the new noises and sensations around her.

She'd be okay, I thought. And she was, for the first little while after we brought her home.

During the first three months, different people came to visit. They all took turns holding her and commented on how alert she was. She seemed interested in everything around her and she looked curiously at people when they spoke to her. She responded positively to Steve and to me and allowed us equal bonding time to feed, change and play with her, most of the time. But those subtle reactions I'd noticed in the hospital still loomed.

Yes, Jaimie let us hold her but only if we'd had her resting on a pillow or blanket over our arms and we needed to be constantly moving—like walking, rocking, or swinging her. She also needed white noise in the background—like running water, a fan blowing, or the sound of an analog television station off-the-air.

Yes, she let us change her clothes and diaper but not without a screeching cry from start to finish. And, yes, she let us play with and talk to her but I noticed whenever Steve spoke to her, she turned her head away from him and squirmed. Then one afternoon, my looming worries grew stronger and I realized we may have had more to worry about than we initially thought.

My afternoon study-time had been interrupted by Jaimie's chirping in the baby monitor. Around that time, Jaimie's night-time sleeping patterns had been horrible. She'd woken up on a nightly basis, somewhere between 2:00 and 3:00 a.m. and literally stayed awake until the sun came up. But, thankfully, she'd allowed herself to sleep during the day.

As I walked down the hallway leading to her room, my stomach tightened. Her fussiness could be so intense some days that even just walking into her room was enough to set her off. We learned quickly that by making extra noise when opening her door or coming near her, she seemed calmer than if we suddenly appeared in front of her.

"Hi Sunshine," I said, opening her door. "Are ya ready to get up now?"

Jaimie didn't look up at me but her little arms and legs flailed around faster the closer I'd gotten to her crib. "Upsy Daisy." I said, gathering her into my arms.

To my surprise, Jaimie cried the second she was in my arms. I checked her diaper—she was still dry. "You must be hungry," I said, rubbing her tummy. "C'mon. Let's get you some num-nums."

By then, her neck was strong enough for me to hold her on my hip, but as soon as I faced her toward me, her body stiffened and she screamed a high-pitched screech that actually rang my eardrums.

"Jaimie, honey, what's wrong?" I said, bouncing her gently. She dug her toes into the top of my jeans and pushed away from me. Her screaming worsened and she grunted each time she pushed on my jeans. It was as if my touch burnt her flesh and facing me scared her.

I tried comforting her one more time. "Sh... sh... it's okay, Jaimie, Mama's here."

Her screaming had gotten so loud I barely heard my own voice. Not knowing what else to do, I put Jaimie back in her crib and stepped back from it... just a little bit. She continued screaming for a few more seconds; then her body relaxed as her crying slowed down, and then stopped.

This couldn't be right, I thought. *Babies weren't supposed to be calmer when you put them down, were they?* And that scenario happened every time we tried picking her up or offering her comfort from that point on.

When I brought these things up with Jaimie's pediatrician he said, "It's natural for a baby to prefer the parent who cares for them most of the time. She'll relax eventually."

I remember thinking, "Just when is this relaxation supposed to happen? People have been telling me that since she was born!"

Even I seemed to trigger negative responses from her. And we couldn't even enjoy normal family activities. Even putting Jaimie in her stroller, if it was too windy (sunny/noisy/smelly/etc.) outside, made her scream. Poor Steve began feeling paranoid just being around Jaimie because even when he'd just said hello to her, she cried. Then Jaimie began teething on top of everything else and all hell broke loose.

We've never been able to figure out what it was about that time that kicked her fussiness into overdrive but gone was our curious, loving, somewhat easy-going girl. As scared as we were of Jaimie's behavior, it was even scarier to believe something more serious could have been wrong with her. What didn't help was that Steve wouldn't jump on board with me to try to get Jaimie help at first.

Steve acknowledged that Jaimie was ornery and that she seemed indifferent to him but he felt I was being overprotective. I knew in my heart he was just as afraid as I was but he'd chosen to deal with it by not dealing with it. And his reaction made me feel even more alone.

"It's becoming exhausting taking care of her, Steve." I said after one of Jaimie's two- hour fits following her bath. "I don't do anything right: she screams all the time; she won't go to sleep unless I rock her and rock her, and I fight with her just to change her diaper. I just don't think this is normal. We should tell the pediatrician about all of this in detail. We need to let him know just how bad things really are."

"And say what?" Steve said. "'Oh my daughter hates her Daddy and everyone else around her'? He'll just tell us that she's making strange or whatever that's called. Isn't that normal for her age? You're the one taking Psychology."

"Look," I said. "These are just textbooks filled with descriptions of abnormal psychological disorders. They don't tell us about Jaimie. There's something wrong, Steve and it's getting worse. I can't even leave the room because she's scared to be apart from me for more than a couple of seconds. I'm really worried."

Steve eased. He cupped my face in his hands and said, "Let's just give it a bit more time, okay? She's getting all these teeth and is just…frustrated. If things don't get better after her teeth come in, we'll tell the doctor."

And we tried. We sat in the pediatrician's office every two months—with Jaimie koala bear-hugging me, screaming at the top of her lungs—trying to convince the doctor something was wrong with her. The scene was the same every time:

He said something like, "You have a very healthy little girl there. Do you have any other concerns?"

I responded with, "Yes, actually. How she's acting right now is a concern. This is how she is most of the time."

He'd answer with, "A lot of children react this way to coming to see the doctor, Chynna. I'm sure you can hear the other little spirited ones down the hall before I come in here."

By that point I would be yelling so the doctor heard me over Jaimie's screaming. Although Steve and I were used to doing it by then, I'm sure the doctor didn't appreciate it. "It isn't just when she comes here. It's at home, at the park, at the grocery store, in the bathtub…"

The conversation always ended with him saying something like, "Chynna, you and Steve are good parents and Jaimie is a very healthy little girl. She's just a little spirited. That's all. She'll grow out of it soon enough."

Just spirited! What really ticked me off during that time was that people weren't listening to us. By listening I don't mean we were dealing with people hard of hearing that we had to repeat ourselves to until they heard us. I mean people simply weren't listening to us. Even the professionals, like Jaimie's doctor or my circle of psychologist friends, weren't listening to us.

Jaimie's behavior was either explained away by the developmental stage she was in at the time or Steve and I were accused of seeing things that weren't there because Jaimie was physically healthy. I just couldn't fathom how people thought we were making it up or even that we were reading more into it. Then Steve hit the nail on the head:

"None of those people live here with her to see what she's really like."

Bingo. Nobody else saw Jaimie getting up—and staying up—every night with night terrors or saw that it took two of us just to change her diaper, or her clothes or witnessed her two to three hour long fits, or saw our pain at not being able to comfort her. Nobody else saw how it ripped Steve's heart out every time Jaimie screamed whenever he got near her. And none of those people had to walk on eggshells not knowing what next event sent Jaimie throwing herself backwards onto the kitchen floor, banging her head into it when she was fine less than one minute earlier.

But how could we convince people that something was wrong when they didn't live with us and only had our word to go by? We needed to prove to them something wasn't right. I had six photo albums full of pictures of Jaimie from when she was born to a year old and in only one of them was she smiling. The others showed hiding her face, screaming at us to put the camera away or, crying. But pictures weren't enough.

We needed more solid proof.

~~~

As Jaimie approached her first year, my heart broke watching her struggle with things other children seemed to enjoy. Most one-year olds explored and were curious about people and what surrounded them. Jaimie did have specific toys that she liked. She enjoyed books, she loved music, bubbles, balls, her soother, and a little beanie Tigger I'd given to her one night in a feeble attempt to calm her. That was pretty much it.

She didn't like most of the stuffed animals she'd gotten. Any toys that were too loud, moved on their own, too bright or had weird textures, she ended up shoving them under her bed or in her closet. And she refused to look at books that were "Scratch-and-Sniff" or textured. When she was very small, she seemed more drawn to odd things like my Tupperware containers or a choo-choo I'd made out of empty Diaper Genie containers. And holidays? Forget about it. Anything like birthdays, Halloween, Easter, and especially, Christmas, where there were decorations involved and changes to things around her, she simply cried inconsolably. She just never seemed to allow herself to enjoy the fun things that other kids did.

I felt so guilty constantly comparing her to other children we saw but what else could I do? Our doctor wasn't seeing what we were and without any other children, who had struggles like Jaimie did, all I could do was take mental notes of what other healthy children were doing. I was desperate to find a solution because Steve and I both noticed Jaimie slipping further into her own world but neither of us knew what to do to draw her back into ours.

I took advantage of my psychology connections by doing research on her behavior. Being a psychology major gave me access to many resources but it was both a blessing and a curse. As a blessing, I could talk to professionals and be given direction for research most other people didn't have access to. As a curse, however, I saw Jaimie's symptoms in every psychological, neurological and emotional disorder out there. One disorder I read the most about was autism.

There were many definitions of autism out there, depending on where one did their research. I learned that autism affected the normal development of the brain, specifically those involved in the areas of social interaction and communication skills. These children showed difficulty in verbal and nonverbal communication, social interactions, and leisure or play activities. Autism also interfered with the ability to communicate and relate to the world around them and the people in it.

Additionally, I learned that children with autism could exhibit repeated body movements (hand flapping, rocking), unusual responses to people or attachments to objects, and resistance to changes in routines. Most worrisome to me was when I read how, in some cases, these children practiced aggressive and/or self-injurious behavior. And that they may experience sensitivities in the five senses (sight, hearing, touch, smell, and taste.)

I was almost positive that Jaimie wasn't autistic. Yes, there were many signs and symptoms she displayed that were similar to children with autism but it's what Jaimie *didn't* have that convinced me it was something else. There were times I looked deep into her ocean blue eyes and saw she was in there. She seemed interested in her world; she just didn't seem to understand how to relate to it. She wasn't speaking but she understood us and did acknowledge us when we spoke to her. And even though she rejected my affection, I felt in my heart that she longed for it.

But the signs and symptoms of autism nagged at me for years later. And, of course, I worried. Each day that passed, Jaimie inverted deeper into herself. And her reactions to situations, experiences, and people grew even scarier.

By the time Jaimie turned one, Steve and I were paranoid to take her anywhere or to allow people to come around her because we didn't know what or who would trigger her fits. It got to the point where dealing with her fits were so exhausting and emotionally draining, we'd have rather avoided situations entirely than to deal with the aftermath—which could linger for days, sometimes up to a week, after an incident.

By then, we had the sense that it was mostly noises, smells, and things touching her that set her off. The problem was we never knew *exactly* what those noises, smells, and touches would be as they seemed to change from day to day. Or her tolerance was different, one way or the other.

We actually had to debrief people before they came to visit: "Okay, here's a list of Do's and Don'ts when dealing with Jaimie. Pay particular attention to numbers one through ten as they involve touching and that's a big no-no. You can't even touch something you want to give to her—you have to just leave it on the table in front of her or give it to Chynna to give to her for you. And for God's sake, don't hug, kiss, cuddle, tickle, talk to, look at, or otherwise interact with her..."

That's a slight exaggeration but I'm sure that's how it must have felt to visitors. Imagine how devastating it was for her Grams who lived two provinces away from us, and only able to see her granddaughter twice a year, to be told to come visit but she couldn't talk to Jaimie, sit beside her, touch her in any way, or even give her something because she'd freak out! And if/when people weren't willing to listen to us or respect Jaimie's space, they simply weren't allowed to come. We just didn't have the patience, energy, or time to explain over and over 'why' when we didn't even know ourselves.

I'm sure people thought we were controlling but we were only trying to keep things calm both for Jaimie as well as for ourselves. Other people just didn't understand that Jaimie couldn't deal with their presence. They didn't understand that it took up to a week, depending on the duration of the visit or the visitor, for her to get over it. And they didn't understand that it was me who had to cope with her reactions on my own since she no longer wanted anything to do with Steve.

I decided after Jaimie's first birthday that I was going to do everything in my power to find someone to listen to us, someone who could give us direction. We simply couldn't do it on our own anymore.

Someone was going to listen to us, damn it!

2 | "Just Spirited" Are You Kidding Me?

The period of time between Jaimie's first and second birthday marked when her reactions to things, people or situations peaked. In fact, her reactions to things became so severe they interfered with everything in her life: eating, sleeping, playing, socializing; even the simple act of changing her clothes or diaper was a battle that took both Steve and I together to achieve.

It was a time of both relief as well as complete frustration. Our frustration stemmed from her becoming completely dependent on me—the one and only person she trusted. I couldn't even go to the bathroom without her crying inconsolably until I came back out. But on the other hand, other people finally witnessed Jaimie's behavior and agreed that something might have been wrong. But her doctor still wasn't convinced.

He still told us not to worry and that she'd grow out of her spirited stage by the time she was two. Was he kidding us? At every doctor's visit, Jaimie's behavior seemed to worsen. It took every restraint inside of me not to grab him and scream, "What is *wrong* with you? Surely this behavior isn't typical of all of your patients!"

We knew that without the doctor's acknowledgement and recommendation we'd never have access to the community resources we needed to find out for sure if something was wrong with

Jaimie. Most community assistance places in Canada—at least here in Edmonton—needed a doctor's referral and without the doctor's referral, we were stuck. Even more frustrating was that the things we were most concerned with were always explained away by something 'behavioral' or 'developmental':

Her slow weight gain: "She's always been long and lean. That's just how she is." (Jaimie was always in the 95th percentile for her height but only between the 15th–25th for her weight.)

The fact that she refused to eat foods she used to like: "All children become pickier as toddlers. She's just exerting her independence."

The fact that she didn't sleep at night: "My children didn't sleep through the night until they were almost five." (Yes, I thought, but did your children wake up with night terrors every night? Or wake up in the middle of the night and stay awake until the sun came up?)

Her severe reactions to smells, sounds, or touch: "Again, she's just trying to be independent. She'll grow out of it."

Her fear of pooping or peeing: "We'll just give her some medicine to help soften her stools; then she won't be able to hold it. As for peeing, just give her a lot to drink and she'll have to go eventually."

Her need for routine and familiarity: "All children need routine and prefer what's familiar to them."

The odd way she handled objects: "Some children simply are fussier with what they choose to play with."

Her aggressive resistance to us trying to get her to do basic hygienic activities, like brushing her hair or teeth, giving her a bath or getting her dressed: "Once again, we can chalk that up to her spiritedness. Most children don't like getting their teeth brushed. These are things she needs to do and will get used to it eventually." It took both Steve and I to do any of these activities, especially getting her dressed. Sometimes, her resistance was so strong, both of us ended up with bruises, bite marks, or scratches all over us.

How she'd hurt herself when she was confused, angry or upset: "Her reactions stem back to her spirited nature. Just be strong and start to administer disciplinary actions."

You get the idea. We were made to feel that everything we were going through was all in our minds. That in order to get Jaimie the help she needed, something very serious had to happen to her or that we at least needed documented proof to convince him. It was angering and my heart broke for poor Jaimie who tried telling us in her own way that she was suffering but no one understood her. That's when I decided to record absolutely everything that went on with Jaimie in a journal. They wanted proof? I made sure they got it.

Essentially we kept track of all of Jaimie's fits—that's what we called her tantrums since "tantrums" didn't quite describe how serious they could be—when they happened; their duration and intensity; what we tried doing to calm her; what worked and what didn't; and, if we were able to figure it out, what triggered them.

That was one of the most difficult chores. Not only did we have to re-live the experiences, we'd read over a situation and think, "Oh my God. This reads like a horror fiction story. Is this really our child?"

It hurt. But at least we felt we were doing something proactive and not just watching from the sidelines. Even though we still didn't have any solid answers, we were able to pinpoint several areas of difficulty and where patterns were established:

Eating: Although Jaimie was never an adventurous eater, she at least tried different things. But as she approached her first birthday, she refused to eat. In fact, it wasn't long before the only things she ate were plain pasta (and it had to be fusilli), a specific kind of chicken pie with all the veggies removed, apples, and vanilla yogurt. For a girl who had trouble keeping weight on, this was a huge concern for us. We'd noticed that she refused foods based on their smell, color, or the way they looked. Whenever we gave her something—even something she'd tried before—she smelled it, poked it, and manipulated it in her hands. If it didn't smell or feel right, she wouldn't eat it. And if we did get her to try something she spat the food out, gagged on it, or threw up right at the table.

Eliminating: The whole process of peeing or pooping seemed to terrify her. If her diaper was even just a tiny bit wet or dirty, she tugged and scratched at it to get it off and would continue tugging and scratching until she was changed. Later on, she'd get us to keep wiping her repeatedly until she felt things were clean enough. It took up to half a wipe box on really bad days!

Pooping was the worst. After she got to one year old, Jaimie held her poop for days. This was a concern not only because it caused discomfort but also because we knew how unhealthy it was. The entire process—whether her poop was soft or hard—terrified her. We knew whenever she needed to go because she ran and hid and when she couldn't hold it any longer, she cried from the moment she started until the moment the clean diaper was back on her.

Later on, toilet training her was a nightmare. She was well over four before she didn't need the Pull-Ups anymore and allowed herself to poop in the toilet. It got to the point where if two full days had passed without her going, we made her sit on the toilet until she did. Of course that never worked—she sat there for hours if you let her. Then we threatened to use a suppository. At three days, we used one and let me tell you…it took days for her to get over that scene. Then, of course, the cycle continued: a feeling of going, holding it for days, threatening, carry through with the treat, fear of going again…

Sleeping: Again, she never slept well. Even as an infant, she needed movement and "white noise" to fall asleep. All I can say is thank goodness we didn't pay for our water in our first apartment because she needed to be rocked by running water to fall asleep!

Starting at about six months, Jaimie started waking up in the middle of the night, screaming and babbling. Because of her age, we'd assumed it was because she wanted a bottle. But there were nights where the action of picking her up to give her one made her screaming worse. By a year, we noticed that sometimes during these awakenings (as we called them), her eyes were open and she looked around but she wasn't really awake. It was disturbing. By two, Jaimie did things like digging, piling her stuffed animals in one part of her bed, or throwing them out, or even covering her ears and screeching. Once she was able to talk, we listened to the frightening conversations she had with someone called, "The Man" who she said told her that terrible things would happen to me if she fell asleep.

Stephen King would have made a lot of money with book ideas in our house during that time. The pattern we found was that the more stressed her day was, the longer she stayed awake, and the worse the awakenings.

Playing: For me this was devastating to watch. Children are supposed to enjoy playing, exploring, and interacting with toys. It's the best part of being a kid! As mentioned earlier, there were certain sorts of toys Jaimie avoided. She stopped playing with toys that made loud, shrill noises; popped up; anything with Velcro; anything that had a scent, or stuffed animals that weren't made from the soft plush material.

She also didn't like sand, dirt, dust, and fluff from carpets or recycled rubber pieces that are sometimes laid down at playgrounds. Oddly, she *did* like playing in the snow. Even when her hands got red and ice cold, she loved playing with it—and eating it! She wasn't very explorative or adventurous. She stuck with toys that were familiar to her and that she knew what to expect from them.

Dressing: When Jaimie was tiny, the only times she didn't scream when we'd dressed her was when we put her in a onesie (those are the short-sleeved shirts that snap up between the legs) and socks. That's it. If you took her socks off, she wouldn't walk on the carpet. If you put pants on her, she screamed until they were taken off. And certain fabrics—like wool, corduroy, or overalls—drove her crazy.

As she got older, it got more challenging to find things she was willing to wear. She refused to wear anything with holes, buttons, zippers, snaps, Velcro, bows, heavy patterns, or bright colors. She wouldn't wear shorts, overalls, skirts, or dresses. Her socks had to be brushed cotton and she would only wear sweats with fleecy insides. And we had to cut the tags out of every single item of clothing—including underwear—or she ripped at the clothing until it was removed.

There were times when Jaimie and I sat on the floor, surrounded by piles of her clothes, as she screamed in frustration with me crying right beside her. By the time she turned two, the only things she allowed us to put on her were tights, long-sleeved shirts, and socks—even in the hottest weather.

Socializing: Quite simply put, she didn't socialize. In fact, if she wasn't who initiated any sort of contact with someone else, she ran away. It didn't matter if it was a woman, man, boy, or girl. I can't tell you how many times I had to run after Jaimie when she sprinted away from the playground just because another child said, "Hello!" to her.

Nevertheless, she seemed interested in people. She pointed at other children playing, or at people doing interesting things. But if they got too close or tried interacting with her, she seemed to panic. Worst was when people actually touched her—that would be when she ran. We thought, maybe, she was just painfully shy but she reacted the same way even to Steve. Sadly, she rarely laughed, smiled, or made eye contact, even with me.

Hurting herself: This was the most upsetting and terrifying part of everything we dealt with in relation to Jaimie's behavior. The main reason I knew something was wrong with her at three months was because it was when her temper surfaced. Even at that young age, Jaimie seemed determined to do things and got extremely angry when she wasn't able to.

I remember watching her, at about three or four months old, trying to crawl—which, according to the baby books, was a bit early. She got up on her hands and knees, rocked back and forth, and then hurled herself forward, landing on her face. After a few attempts, she simply lay on her side and screamed with her little body stiff as a board, her fists clenched and her skin a bright crimson. Then she rolled back over and kept trying. She did it but her fierce determinism was disturbing… almost obsessive! And it got worse as she got older.

By the time she was a year old, Jaimie resorted to clawing her skin, scratching her eyes, pulling her hair out in clumps, even smashing her head into the floor, wall, or her headboard. Usually it stemmed from frustration but we noticed her doing such things after we'd touched her or if her clothes bothered her or even when we cooked certain things. And if we got a new toy that was too noisy, moved too much, or she otherwise didn't like, she simply threw it into her closet.

Her anger and aggression almost never resulted from her not getting her way but more from what surrounded her.

Communicating: By the time she was two, Jaimie had hardly spoken a word. I'd taught her some simple sign language gestures to indicate things like, "drink," "tired," "hungry," "soother," and similar words. But she didn't even use the gestures much. A lot of times, she simply went and got what she wanted/needed, except, of course for things she wanted to eat or drink. When we tried getting down to her level to ask, "What do you want, Jaimie? Do you want ____ or ____ or____…" she got even more upset.

Yes, there was the frustration of not being understood on her part but it was as if our response to her, our interacting with her, upset her even more. In fact, when she got too upset, she simply shut down. She completely zoned out—as we called it—not even acknowledging us. In that state of mind, she was unreachable and unresponsive. It was frightening.

Aside from the above instances—and even though she wasn't talking—there were times where life with her seemed almost normal. As mentioned earlier, she loved books. She also loved drawing and doing puzzles, both of which she was able to do from a very young age. She found great comfort in music (especially classical, jazz, the Beatles, and the Wiggles) and danced along. And when you spoke to her, you could tell she heard you and absorbed your words. She just never responded.

Clearly our Jaimie was intelligent and found enjoyment in certain activities—which is why I'd always questioned her being autistic. So the question I asked myself was: *What was causing her to shut us out?*

I had to find out, even if I didn't like the answer.

3 | Steve's Story: "Daddy Loves You"

Daddies are role models to their sons. They help to guide boys to be respectable, hard-working men. To their little girls, Daddies are the 'first man' in their lives. Girls learn how men are supposed to treat them and what will and won't be tolerated. There are so many men out there who miss out on being a father to their children—either by choice or because they're prevented from playing that role. So, it was important to me to be with a man who would take his role as a father very seriously. Steve was that man.

Daddies are a very important part of their children's lives. As a girl who grew up without her father, I felt very much what I must have missed as I watch Steve with our four children. Steve is an amazing father. It may have a lot to do with the fact he didn't enjoy a close relationship with his own father but he's always tried to be a hands-on Dad. And, believe me, it's been a difficult journey for him at times.

There's something about Steve that Jaimie wasn't able to handle. In fact, we still haven't figured out what it might be. Whether it's his scent, the tone of his voice, or the feel of his skin, but after spending any small amount of time with him, she ends up screaming, "Daddy, go away!" The worst part has been watching him withdraw from his own child because he didn't want to make things worse.

When we first brought Jaimie home from the hospital, Steve did everything: diaper changes, walked and rocked her to sleep, even dealt with projectile vomit situations. But at around three months, when Jaimie started teething, things changed. She simply wanted nothing to do with him. She screamed at his touch; turned her head whenever he spoke to her; and wouldn't even take her bottle if he tried feeding her.

How awful it must have been for him to only hold her for about five or ten minutes to give me a break—and, even then, he had to hold her with a pillow between them or she tried wriggling out of his arms—before having to give her back to me. Of course, as soon as she was back with me, or he put right down, she settled. When she got older—between one and two years of age— she was more aggressive about her feelings towards him. She pushed him; yelled at him to leave her alone or to let her go; covered her ears when he spoke; gagged when he got too close; and threw her cup at him when he tried to just give her juice or milk.

We didn't understand why. It was one thing to prefer one parent over the other, as our physician stated happened often. But it was just not normal for a child to reject a loving parent outright. And Steve gave up. He basically backed off and let me deal with her most of the time. In his mind, it was better to have stayed in the background than to have made things even worse.

After a while, I wondered why we'd even had a child when we couldn't share in raising her or even loving her. But I admired Steve's strength. Most guys would have said, "Why the hell even stay, then." and left. He didn't. He did his best with what he could do, even when it hurt. God love him.

After Jaimie's SPD diagnosis, when she was about two-and a half, we began therapy as a family. It taught us how to communicate and relate to Jaimie as well as helped her learn more effective coping tools to deal with us. Unfortunately, Steve often felt like an outsider both because Jaimie still rejected his 'Daddy-ness' and also because he wasn't always able to participate in her one-on-one therapy sessions.

One evening, not too long after Jaimie began her in-home therapy with her occupational therapist (OT), Steve and I had made a date to catch up. We hadn't seriously talked for quite a while and things between us seemed…strained. He'd always been so quiet and had never been very open about his feelings. But I knew he'd been hurting even if he'd never shown it outwardly. He simply hid behind jokes.

After having done Jaimie's bedtime ritual three times, until she felt safe and satisfied, I came downstairs for our chat. Steve sat on the couch, hiding his face behind the newspaper.

"You want to talk now?" I asked.

He put his newspaper down. "Yeah, sure. Tell me what's going on."

"There's not much to tell, really," I said. "Donna, Jaimie's OT gave me this questionnaire to fill out. I'm supposed to rate Jaimie's reactions to situations, people, and other stuff. God, I don't know about this. I hope we're doing the right thing."

"We have to try, hun," Steve said, picking his paper back up. "What's the questionnaire for?"

"It's something we're supposed to do together," I said. "It's going to tell us what Jaimie's tolerance level is for her environment so we know what sort of treatment to get her."

"Great," he said from behind the front page.

I shook my head at him. "No wonder Jaimie is so indifferent with you. You show absolutely no interest in her well-being. You know what? Forget it. Read your paper and I'll just take care of it by myself. Like always."

He threw the newspaper to the side, startling me. "What am I *supposed* to do," he bellowed. "I can't touch her or she screams. I tell her I love her and she says 'no, only Mama.' I can't even comfort her and my being around just seems to make things worse. Tell me, Chynna, what do I do?"

I had seen him cry just three times in the ten years that we had been together: when his grandmother died; when Jaimie was born; and right then. For the first time during all the madness, he'd finally let his emotions flow. I was proud of him.

I sat beside him, guiding his head onto my lap; then stroked his hair as I said, "You tell her you love her even if she doesn't want to hear it. You give her your support even if it's from a distance because she can't handle your touch. And you tell her you're here for her even if she doesn't want you to be. You're her daddy and she needs to know she can feel safe with you. You can't be afraid to show your feelings—that won't help her. Show her it's okay to be scared or angry or sad and that you feel those things too."

I wasn't sure if what I'd said made him feel better about the situation. How does one make someone feel *better* about their child rejecting them? You can't. I had been the only person in Jaimie's world whom she'd trusted near her to do the things she'd needed done. Even though I'd never received physical love from Jaimie either—because hugs, cuddles, and kisses were out of the question for a girl who couldn't handle touch—she'd never pushed me away. I could only imagine how difficult and painful it had been for Steve. I'd felt helpless for years—stuck between the two people I'd loved most in the world and not being able to help either of them.

Then at bedtime the next night, I guided Jaimie up the stairs to her bedroom. Steve reached out to her as she'd rushed past him on her way to the stairs and he said, "Goodnight, Jaimie. Daddy loves you."

Jaimie stopped dead in her tracks, her eyes widening. "No, you don't say that. You don't love me. Only Mama."

Steve held his ground—he didn't back down nor shied away. "Yes, Mama loves you, Jaimie. But Daddy loves you too. It's okay if you don't want to hear it but Daddy wants to say it."

To this day, Jaimie still hasn't told Steve she loves him. But she knows her Daddy loves her. And she shows him in her own ways: she draws pictures for him, she tells him about her day, and asks him about his and will even sit in his lap—facing away from him, but still a huge step.

One day, she'll be brave enough to say, "I love you too, Daddy." Until that day, Steve knows in his heart how she feels. And he never lets a day go by that he doesn't remind her of his love for her.

...And Baby Makes Four: The Confirmation

Shortly before Jaimie turned one, Steve and I talked about having more children. It was a concept that terrified both of us. Aside from the usual concerns of whether we could afford it or if we had enough room, we asked ourselves a lot of other questions: What if we had another child with the same temperament as Jaimie? Would we be able to give the same attention to both children? Could I handle caring for an infant when Jaimie needed me so much? And, what concerned us most was whether Jaimie would be able to handle another baby in our house.

We were told that because of the level of difficulty we'd had conceiving Jaimie, we'd have to start early for another child as we might have the same problems. Imagine our surprise when the stick turned blue after just two months of trying! I was so shocked I had to do the test again—twice! Elation swept over me, then despair. What was I going to do?

I left one of the positive pregnancy tests on top of Steve's dresser for him to find when he came home from work that day. I just couldn't bring myself to say the words, "I'm pregnant." Of course, he never saw it. We carried on an entire conversation about his day until Jaimie reached up on her tip toes and tried grabbing it.

He took the test from Jaimie's hand, and then took a closer look at her find. "Really?" he said, looking at me.

I nodded then burst into tears. I don't know why. I tried never to cry in front of Jaimie because it scared her. It wasn't hormones. I started thinking about how life would be when the baby came when I was already drained, tired, and stressed. Not a good way to start.

He came over and gave me one of his famous bear hugs. "Oh, honey," he said. "Everything will be okay. I'm sure. You should be happy. I'm the one that should be ticked off. I only got two tries in before it worked. That's so unfair!"

Leave it to Steve to turn my frown upside down. I knew we'd be okay—eventually. And I also knew it wasn't good to worry so early on.

I was very sick for the first five months of the pregnancy. This was unacceptable to Jaimie, who was used to me jumping to her every need when it was demanded. As my baby bump grew, so did Jaimie's tantrums and our concerns for her.

One night, about five months into the pregnancy, I was awakened by a steady thumping noise on our bedroom wall. It was similar to the sound of a bouncing ball. I crept into Jaimie's room, as that's where the sound came from, and found Jaimie in her crib ramming her head into her headboard. I had no idea how long she'd been at it but her head-banging was so strong she had moved her crib practically across the room.

Night frights were nothing new. Nor was her banging her head on the wall. But doing it in her sleep was new and it scared me. I rushed over to shove something between her head and the headboard only to find everything in her bed on the floor. The weird thing was her bed toys weren't just tossed around; they were neatly lined up beside where her bed had been. The head banging got harder so I instinctively tried shoving my hand between her head and the headboard only to curse out loud at the impact.

I must have startled her because she stopped suddenly and turned to me. I'll never forget the look on her little face: eyes wide open, a goose egg – the size of a large marble – on her forehead and her face shiny from tears and drool. She screamed, stood up, then head-butted me in the belly. She knocked the wind out of me but, at the time, I was more concerned that Jaimie would knock herself unconscious than whether she'd hurt the baby.

After about an hour, it was over. She lay back down and I watched her until I saw her back slowly raise and fall. It was then that I realized I hadn't felt the baby move since before I went into Jaimie's room.

I lay on the couch for several minutes until I finally felt a hearty kick in my side. Then I cried until the sun came up. In the morning, I told Steve everything that had happened and I'm not sure whether he completely believed me. But he was scared too, especially for me and the baby.

"That's it," he said. "There's no way she can be allowed to do that. What if next time she hurts the baby? Or you?"

"It's fine," I said. "Don't worry about it. She didn't do it on purpose. She was asleep."

He shook his head at me. "What if next time she does it when she's awake?" he asked. "You can't do everything all by yourself. Not right now."

I knew he was right but what was I supposed to do? The only time I'd left her with Steve since she'd been born was when I had to write an exam for university. And although they survived, it didn't go as well as I'd hoped it would.

When I'd gotten home from that exam, there was a note that Steve had taken Jaimie to run around in the field behind our apartment building. We'd done that a lot whenever Jaimie had trouble napping or seemed to need to work off some excess energy. I'd gone out to meet them. From a distance, I'd seen Steve walking a safe distance behind Jaimie as she ran around in circles with her arms flapping. Steve had tried picking her up and she'd reacted by throwing herself backwards, screaming.

As she'd kicked her feet at him, screaming, "No! Want Mama!" I remember walking faster toward them, then running as fast as a woman could at thirty-five weeks pregnant. By the time I'd gotten to her, she was too far gone for me to calm. There we all were in the middle of the field, Jaimie screeching on her back with her legs and arms flailing; Steve staring at her with his hands on his hips; and me on my knees waiting for an opening to try to get her to listen to me. So I did the only thing I knew that worked: I sang to her Paul McCartney's classic song "Blackbird."

She didn't calm down completely but I saw in her eyes that she'd heard me. When that didn't work, I sang Wiggles songs, hummed Mozart; heck, I even threw in a Michael Bublé song or two. After about half-an hour, she calmed enough for us to take her home and put down for a rest. Once I put her to bed, I laid down too. I didn't tell Steve this but after my sprint in the field, I started experiencing cramps and false labor (and continued to until I went into full labor a couple of weeks later.)

After that incident, I silently promised two things: That I'd always be there for Jaimie, even if I had to give up my own things; and second, if I couldn't figure out what was wrong with her, I'd do what I could to calm her. And boy, did we need to do a lot of calming over the next few weeks.

We tried our best to prepare Jaimie for the arrival of the new baby. We did all the regular things they'd recommended in the parenting/baby magazines. We tried getting her to choose small items for the baby's crib; put her in charge of choosing the outfit to bring the baby home in; and even helping Daddy put together the baby's bed. But, seriously, you can only prepare a not-even-two-year old so much. How much did she truly understand?

All Jaimie knew was that whatever was in my tummy prevented me from doing things the way I used to. And she didn't like it. Whenever the baby moved in my tummy, we tried preparing her by saying things like, "Look Jaimie! Baby is moving. Do you want to feel it?"

But whenever we'd put her hand on my tummy to feel the baby move, Jaimie jumped then smacked my belly. She didn't understand. She was just reacting to the weird feeling of a something squirming that she couldn't see—I knew that. But if she reacted that intensely to the baby when it wasn't even with us yet, how was she going to react to a newborn's cries? Or to dirty diapers? Or to the fact that Mama would need to pay a lot of attention to the new baby? The entire situation ripped me apart every day.

I never even got to enjoy being pregnant. I was riddled with guilt: about being pregnant; about not being able to be the Mama I'd been before I got pregnant; about not being there for Jaimie when I'd had to go into the hospital to give birth; even about bringing home the new baby into our chaotic world. Heck, I even felt guilty bonding with the new baby. Those thoughts simmered inside of me throughout the entire pregnancy. Despite everything, Jordhan, our second daughter, arrived on October 1, 2004. And it was during Jordhan's birth that I was reminded there were other things I needed to pay attention to.

I thought about Jaimie the entire time I was in the delivery room. I left for the hospital in the middle of the night—right around when Jaimie woke up with a night terror—when my contractions got so bad I wasn't able to stand up through them. I remember I'd looked in her room just before running downstairs to catch a cab, thinking, "Please God. Please let her be okay with everything. Help her to allow Steve to take care of her."

I knew Steve would do his best to care for Jaimie. And he kept telling me they'd survive. That didn't make me feel any better. I didn't want them just to survive. I wanted us to be like every other family who only had to worry about a bit of sibling jealousy. I wanted to feel good about leaving Steve with his daughter. And I wanted Jaimie to feel good about being alone with her daddy. None of those things were a reality for us, though. And I didn't know what to do about it or even how to try to fix things.

Even though the labor and birth was a much easier and shorter process the second time around, Jordhan went into distress because her umbilical cord was wrapped around her neck. The doctor had trouble getting her unwound. For a good five minutes, I laid there panting with the oxygen mask on my face as the doctor tried as quickly and gently as she could to free Jordhan. At one point, my nurse prayed for Jordhan because they'd lost her heartbeat—just like what had happened with Jaimie! Finally, I was allowed to push again and felt a wave of relief as Jordhan slid out of me.

When my doctor placed Jordhan in my arms, I was finally able to enjoy her. My love bubbled up and overflowed as I cried for several minutes. I even got to cut Jordhan's umbilical cord because the birth happened so fast, Steve missed the event. All of these things I took as signs of good things to come. Right then, I knew there was a reason for Jordhan being in our lives. It was a miracle we'd had Jaimie and Jordhan's presence was no less of one.

"I don't know how, my little Jordy," I said to Jordhan as she gripped my thumb. "But, I just know you were meant to be here. And I have a feeling it's for Jaimie. I just hope she sees you that way."

A few hours later, Jordhan and I were taken to a hospital room where we waited for Steve and Jaimie. I was so nervous. I'd called Steve after I'd had Jordhan and heard Jaimie screaming for me in the background. He'd told me she wouldn't even let him get her morning cup of milk or let him get her dressed. But I guess, with some prompting of being able to see Mama and the new baby, she eventually let him because they'd gotten to the hospital safe and sound.

I had my lunch tray sitting on a table and Jordhan slept soundly in her bassinette. As soon as Steve opened the door to my room, Jaimie sprinted toward me and leapt up onto the bed. The first thing she did was crawl toward the bassinette, pulled herself up and leaned into it. As Jaimie moved closer down to Jordhan's face, I moved to grab her but then I heard her little voice, "Hi baby. I Jaimie."

I was stunned. The only other words Jaimie had said before that were "Mama," "Soodee," (her name for her pacifier), and "Ducky Guy." (One of the Wiggles' dancers.)

"When did she start saying that?" I asked Steve.

He smiled. "Just now."

Right then, I knew Jordhan was there for Jaimie. I'd always felt Jaimie needed another person to help her feel safe in her world; to make her see that things don't have to be so scary all the time; a friend—besides me—who'd make her feel brave. In the years to come, my early prediction solidified but it took quite a while for Jaimie to see Jordhan as an ally and a blessing.

Jaimie wasn't able to handle Jordhan's crying. Whenever Jordhan did cry—and thank goodness it wasn't often—Jaimie sat in the middle of the floor, rocking with her hands over her ears screaming until Jordhan stopped. If we changed a diaper, Jaimie coughed and gagged for almost an hour after the event. And when I fed Jordhan, Jaimie got very angry. In fact, it got to the point where we'd have to cover Jordy's head whenever Jaimie came around because Jaimie tried to punch her in the head. And if I paid more attention to Jordhan than Jaimie felt necessary, she tried pulling the baby right out of my arms. But it wasn't always so bad.

Jaimie loved running to get diapers or outfits for Jordhan. She liked lying on the floor beside her for floor fun time. She even enjoyed climbing into Jordhan's crib with Jordhan when I got her after a nap. But what amazed us was even though Jaimie wasn't able to handle most things about babies, Jaimie only smiled or laughed with Jordhan. And she was the only person Jaimie gave hugs to.

I also finally had more proof for Jaimie's doctor. Jordhan was a very different baby than Jaimie was. Jordhan loved to be kissed, hugged, and cuddled. She laughed and cooed. She interacted with us and made eye contact with us right from the start. She seemed interested in the activities going on around her and, most importantly, she *loved* being with her Daddy. Jordhan was exactly how babies were supposed to be. Sure she cried once in a while and was cranky but it was tolerable. *Normal.* We finally knew for sure something was wrong with Jaimie.

Unfortunately, things had to get worse before they could get better.

5 | The Last Straw

In July of 2005, we'd outgrown our tiny two-bedroom apartment and decided that we'd make the move into a three bedroom townhouse. Moving can be a stressful situation for anyone. For someone who's moved many times during her life, I can honestly say the best thing about moving was unpacking. The worst parts are over: finding a truck, packing up, loading, finding friends who'd actually be willing to help you on a long weekend—which it was when we moved. But once you can unpack your stuff, you're home. Of course, that's the best-case scenario for people who move without toddlers. And without a toddler who'd developed an intense need for things to stay the same.

Packing with Jaimie around was a nightmare. Every time I wrapped something up and put it in a box, she came right behind me and unpacked it.

"No!" she said. "No go."

Then she put whatever I dared to pack away back where it belonged. We had to do most of our packing when Jaimie was asleep; then we sent the packed boxes over to a friend of Steve's who stored them in his garage until move day. I felt so sorry for Jaimie. First, we brought this new baby into the house she had to share everything with; then we were packing up all of our things into a brand new home.

In the end, Jaimie handled everything okay. We distracted her by allowing her to drive our things with Steve in the moving truck. She liked that. But when we got to our new home, Jaimie demanded her stuff come out first. And we had to put everything in her new room exactly as it had been set up in her old room. That wasn't the end of it either.

Even though the rest of us had settled into our new home, Jaimie still struggled with the changes. Her need for routine and what was familiar to her became even more intense. In fact, if we were going through her bedtime routine, we needed to do the entire process from the start if we missed even just one step. It was exhausting. Even if I did everything exactly the way she wanted, she still got up with night frights, or wanted to be with me.

Shortly after our move, I began researching for more information on Jaimie's behavior. I've always been a person who can handle anything as long as I have all the resources and information to draw from. When I had cervical cancer, I talked to other women and I researched it so it wouldn't be as scary. When I found out about my bicornuate uterus, I read journals and asked endless questions to my doctor so I'd know what was going on inside of me. But without knowing for sure what was going on with Jaimie, all I could do was research her behaviors or symptoms and match them to…something. I certainly didn't want to label my child but, darn it, I needed to help her. How was I supposed to do that when I didn't know what I was fighting?

I sought out other mothers of autistic children because, until then, all I knew about autism was how it was represented on television or in books: a socially recluse child, rocking to calm him or herself and freaking out to any sort of effort someone makes to interact with him or her. Of course, this was as wrong as anyone who'd made snap judgments about Jaimie's behavior. So, I read more about it and asked many questions.

I was immediately embraced into this cyberspace community of mothers having children with special needs. They gave Steve and me things we'd never had before then: acceptance, guidance, advice, and direction. It was a true relief for me, most of all, to know that there were people who got my concerns and never once made me feel crazy for feeling the way I did. And, even through the Internet—without never having met me or seen Jaimie—felt my concerns were justified enough to need extra help.

They sent me wonderful resources and books, which I eagerly read. The only two things I found even close to describing the way Jaimie acted was, again, autism and another neurological disorder called Asperger's. There are literally hundreds of books and other resources on these two subjects. In the newer resources I'd found since I'd last researched the subject I read that children with autism usually display varying degrees of the following signs and symptoms:

- Expressive and receptive communication and social deficits.
- Insistence on routine and resistance to change.
- Appearing to be "off in their own little world."
- Resistance to physical closeness, such as hugging.
- Attachment to "odd" toys, such as kitchen utensils.
- Parallel play (playing beside other children rather than interactively with them) and lack of imaginative play.
- Sudden and apparently unexplainable angers and tantrums.
- Repetitive behaviors and obsessive-compulsive disorder.
- Splinter skills (excelling in a particular skill that is above the apparent IQ level.

- Appearing to have sensory overload in normal situations.

(Taken from *The Everything Parent's Guide to Children with
Autism* by Adelle Jameson Tilton)

This list was much more informative and geared to the layman
so it was easier for me to relate them to our situation. All I could
think of after reading that list was, "Wow! This is *totally*
Jaimie!" But the more I researched autism, the less sure I still was
that it was Jaimie's problem. What I didn't know from my earlier
research was that in order for children to be categorized as
autistic, they also had to display deficits in other areas, such as
developmentally and cognitively, which Jaimie didn't show. In
fact, she was developmentally ahead in many areas. Then, I read
all the information about Asperger's Syndrome.

In that disorder, a child has to be impaired socially in more
than one of the following areas:

- Impairment in the use of nonverbal behaviors (such
  as eye contact, facial expressions, and gestures)
  during social interaction.

- Lack of development of relationships with peers.

- Failure to seek to share enjoyment, interests, or
  achievements with other people (for example, by not
  showing objects of interest to others.)

- Failure to reciprocate emotions or social gestures.

On top of that, a child also has to demonstrate "restrictive
repetitive and stereotyped patterns of behaviors, interests and
activities," in at least one of the following areas:

- Unusually intense preoccupation with one or more
  stereo-typed interests.

- Obsessively following specific, nonfunctional routines
  or rituals.

- Repeated motions, such as hand or finger flapping or
  twisting.

- Unusual preoccupation with parts of objects.

In both cases, their behaviors have to be significant enough to interfere with normal living. One thing I found confusing about these disorders was that there are so many different versions underneath the headings of autism or Asperger's making one feel like a new branch was created whenever a child showed signs or symptoms that didn't fit neatly in a specific category. I decided at that point that shoving what I'd learned to the back of my mind again and putting my focus on what I could do for Jaimie was more important than trying to give her a label.

My greatest fear was because my mother had bipolar disorder and her birth father died of Alzheimer's Disease. *Did Jaimie have something wrong with her brain? What if I'd unknowingly passed something on to my child?*

I wanted to pay closer attention to what she was doing, how she was or wasn't functioning to see what direction we could go in. One frosty morning, about three months after we'd moved into our new home, it became crystal clear we were losing the battle of trying to care for Jaimie on our own. Whatever tried grabbing control of our little girl came out in full force. And it scared the hell out of me.

I just knew that day was going to be a huge challenge from the moment we'd woken up. As usual, Jaimie had woken up before six a.m. Her eyes bore dark purple circles under them as her sleep had been interrupted by hourly night frights.

It had taken forever but she'd finally chosen clothes that felt right—no tags, zippers, buttons, or funny feelings. When she'd gotten downstairs to the living room, she'd seen her milk in her sippie cup, as always, and the television on the weather channel. She never actually watched the television but some days she needed extra noise in the room to block out the noises she couldn't handle, such as Jordhan's budgie-like squeaks and giggles.

Jaimie's tired blue eyes darted back and forth from Jordhan to the television. I knew I needed to get her away from that environment for a while. I'd decided that a walk before lunch was the best way to cool us all off and clear our heads. It had taken us over half an hour to get ready for the fall weather: jackets, shoes, mitts, and several diaper changes. We'd finally left the house. But no sooner had we turned the corner of our block than Jaimie froze in her tracks saying, "Mama, my bum tickles."

At almost three years old, Jaimie still wore diapers because she wasn't ready for the toilet training process. Actually, she was ready and we tried many times. She knew when she had to go so it wasn't that she didn't understand the process of going to the bathroom, or that she wasn't able to control her pee or poop. The problem was that she controlled it *too much*. She wouldn't allow herself to go—even with her diaper on. She was stuck between not liking the feeling of going but hating a wet or dirty diaper. So she held it. And that, of course, created even more discomfort.

Her wearing diapers never bothered us. A lot of kids were difficult to toilet train. But it was a huge battle to change her too. From the moment you ripped the diaper tabs to open the diaper she covered her ears and screamed. Then she kicked at you when you wiped her. A person only needed to get booted a few times in the face before giving up! And because you couldn't clean her well enough she complained that she was itchy. That must have been what happened that day.

I'd taken a deep breath and said, "Jaimie, honey, I wiped you several times before we left the house. Let's keep going. I'm sure the feeling will go away." Jordhan whined, not understanding why we'd stopped.

Jaimie's breathing had gotten faster. "No. Can't do it. My bum tickles. My need to go home." As usual, I didn't understand what to do to help her.

"Jaimie, *please...*," was all I'd gotten out before Jaimie covered her ears, threw herself on the ground and screamed. Then

Jordhan joined her. Angry tears filled my eyes—partly because it had taken so long to get ready and then we had to go back already and partly because I simply had no clue what was wrong.

I grabbed Jaimie's arm. She made her body go limp like a rag doll. It had taken all my strength to hold her so she wouldn't whack her head on the cement. I yanked her to a standing position then dragged her back to the house kicking and screaming as Jordhan screamed in stereo from my hip.

I'd unlocked the door continuing to drag Jaimie back into the house. I put both girls down, and then decided who to help first. Both girls screamed at the top of their lungs: one reaching out desperately to me while the other lay on her back kicking the floor and pulling her hair out.

"Wipe my bum, Mama. Make itch stop!" Jaimie screamed.

I took Jordhan's shoes and jacket off so she wouldn't overheat while I dealt with Jaimie. Then I approached Jaimie slowly, telling her exactly what I had to do: "Mama has to take off your jacket and shoes, Jaimie. Then I can stop the itch, okay?"

"No! No touch me!" she shrieked. She'd never talked to me like that before. I was frightened.

"Mama has to touch you if you want me to stop the itch, Jaimie. So, just…" I was silenced. Jaimie kicked me in the face. A metallic flavor flooded my mouth. I wiped my mouth on the back of my hand, which left behind a trail of blood.

"Noooooooooooo! No touch me!" Jaimie screamed again. Poor Jordhan was so upset by the whole scene her cries were almost silent.

I'd forced Jaimie to face me by grabbing her arms and I said, over her screaming, "Calm down, Jaimie. Just tell me what you want! Why can't you just tell me?"

My actions only made things even worse as I'd done the forbidden: I'd touched her. I'd managed to get her shoes and pants off before trying to take off her diaper. No sooner had I gotten it off, Jaimie stood up and urinated on the carpet.

"Jaimie!" I yelled. "There is no excuse for that!"

"AHHH!!" Jaimie threw herself backwards; then repeatedly whacked her head against the floor. I scrambled, searching for something to cushion the blows as the hits got harder and harder.

"Ah...ah...ah....ah..." she grunted with each strike.

I'd found a towel close by and shoved it under Jaimie's head. She let out one long scream as though she'd been exercised and the demon left her body. Then she just lay on her back, staring at the ceiling.

In that moment, I saw things from the outside for the first time. There was Jaimie, with her hair soaked and matted to her head from sweat, her tears and her nose running all over her face; Jordhan, screamed herself almost to sleep, and cowered in the corner of the room; and me, nursing a fat, cut lip and urine on me and the floor.

It was clear that Jaimie was not just a spirited little girl and something needed to be done.

No more procrastination.

~~~

After getting both girls down for a needed nap, I sat with my hands wrapped around a nice hot mug of chamomile tea waiting for Steve's daily after-lunch phone call. My lip stung, my eyes burned and my heart ached.

I interrupted the phone's first ring. "Hello?"

"Hey gorgeous. How's it..." was all I let Steve get out before I burst into tears again. I recounted what happened, then waited for his response.

"Hello? Are you still there?" I sniffed. I was sniffed at in response.

He spoke in a loud whisper. "Oh my God, hun. What are we going to do?"

"We need to help her, Steve," I said. "And we need to do it now. No more waiting. No more excuses."

"Call the doctor," he said. "I'll get the time off work."

As I dialed Dr. Morriarty's number, I remembered the urine drying into our carpet and I still hadn't changed my clothes.

Nothing else seemed to matter.

~~~

I got an emergency appointment with Jaimie's pediatrician a few days later. Steve and I shared our concerns but we couldn't look at each other—our tears would have made it impossible to get the story out. I told the doctor what had happened a few days before and he finally agreed Jaimie needed help.

"Sounds like she has a bit of a behavioral problem," he said, writing notes on Jaimie's chart.

That was it. I'd had it. "A *bit* of a behavioral problem?" I said. "Getting angry because I won't let her have candy or a toy is a 'bit of a behavioral problem'. Kicking me in the face, hitting her head on the floor until she practically passes out, refusing to get dressed because tags hurt her, not wanting us to touch her—these are more than just behavioral problems. And just look at her"—I gestured to my lap as Jaimie sat with her back to everyone, cling to me— "this is how I spend most of my damn day."

Steve squeezed my hand. The doctor stared at me for a second, and then cleared his throat. "I'm so sorry. Let's get you some contacts to call, okay?"

"Thank you," I whispered.

I filled out information forms for programs Jaimie could get into and the nurse gave me a phone number for an Edmonton Early Intervention Program (EEIP).

"You poor thing," she said. "This must be so hard on you." She squeezed my arm, assuring me she'd fax off the papers to the facility that day and someone would contact me soon.

I hoped 'soon' was the next day.

~~~

An early Intervention Program Coordinator from the EEIP (Edmonton Early Intervention Program), named Maria, came over the following week. It was just Jaimie, Jordhan, and me because Steve couldn't get out of work. It marked the first of many meetings we'd have on our road to finding Jaimie help.

How it worked was that a coordinator was usually sent to assess the severity of the situation; then a recommendation for treatment was made. Maria asked me what seemed like hundreds of questions. I didn't mind though; it was such a relief having someone listen to me. After I told her about Jaimie's struggles with eating and going to the bathroom, she stopped writing in her notebook and said, "Poor Jaimie...to struggle even with the basic functions of life. Why didn't you come to us sooner?"

I broke down. "Because I didn't know about you. Plus, we needed a doctor's referral and he didn't believe there was a problem until recently."

She shook her head. "Did he know Jaimie barely eats anything and, if she is given food, it has to be set a specific way on her plate?"

I nodded.

"Wow," she said, rolling her eyes. "Unfortunately we hear that a lot. If something can't be reduced to a medical explanation, it's psychological. Don't worry. We know about Jaimie now and we'll do the best we can to help her."

After we chatted a bit longer, she told me she wanted to set up another meeting with one of their top occupational therapists, (OT) Donna Gravelle. We set up something for the following week to give Jaimie some time in between visits.

On the OT appointment day, Jaimie ran to the door to see Maria. But when Jaimie saw Maria wasn't alone, she ran back to the living room. After introductions were made and Donna played with Jordhan for a bit, she entered the living room to introduce herself to Jaimie. Maria observed the interactions from the couch and I stationed myself on the floor with Jordhan where Jaimie could still see me.

"Hi Jaimie," Donna said. Jaimie ignored her. "I'm going to do a few things with Jaimie to see how she reacts, okay?" Donna whispered to me. "I won't do anything that hurts her, I promise. I just want to see her tolerance level."

"That's fine," I said. Donna sat beside Jaimie on the floor, who played with her trains, talking to herself. Donna brushed her hand against Jaimie's. Jaimie withdrew her hand but didn't cry. There was no break in Jaimie's talking or playing—it was as though none of the rest of us were there.

Donna pointed a few things out to me as she worked with Jaimie. "Watch this," she said moving closer to Jaimie. Jaimie talked faster and her movements were more rapid the closer Donna got to her. As Donna moved further away, Jaimie's speech slowed down and she seemed more relaxed.

"Did you see that?" Donna asked.

Jaimie's reactions were more than familiar. "Yeah," I said. "She's been doing that since she was a baby. It's gotten worse since Jordhan has become mobile and tries to go over to try playing with her. What does it mean?"

"I can't make a solid diagnosis right now but I have a suspicion of what's going on here," she said. "I'm positive Jaimie has Sensory Processing Disorder." (Note: At the time of Jaimie's diagnosis, SPD was called Sensory Integration Dysfunction or SID. Because of the confusion between SID and SIDS, it became Sensory Processing Disorder or SPD. This name change also symbolizes the recognition that it's an actual disorder effecting overall daily functioning and not just an illness or dysfunction.)

Those seven words punched me right in the stomach. The demon inside Jaimie—who'd lived with us for the past two-and-a-half years, and I fought with every day—now had a name.

Now we can fight you fair and square!

The only thing was I had no idea what SPD was. "What is this SPD? Is it a form of autism?"

"No," Donna said, "Although autistic children do have sensory sensitivities. The best way to explain it to you is like this: For most of us, sensory integration is normal. That's when our brain takes in information from around us, processes it then sends messages to the body on what to do with that information. Jaimie, here, doesn't have this sensory integration. When her brain takes in the information, it gets 'scrambled' and it doesn't understand how to read those messages. Because it can't read them, it doesn't know what to do with them, which causes confusion. And that's why Jaimie breaks down."

I supposed I looked totally confused because Donna laughed and said, "I know it's a lot to understand. All you need to know is that it's my job to help Jaimie learn how to cope with her SPD and to help her to learn the tools she needs to be able to do things that other kids enjoy...just in a new way."

I eased. "Will this go away?"

"No," Donna said. "She'll always have SPD. But it seems to be the worst during these preschool years when the communication skills aren't quite developed. Once she learns how to communicate better, things will feel safer to her and she most likely won't break down as much."

She handed me a book called, *The Out Of Sync Child: Recognizing and Coping with Sensory Integration Dysfunction*, by Carol Stock Kranowitz. "This will give you a lot of the answers you need. Try to read it over before the next time I come and if you have any more questions then, we'll have a chat. Never be afraid to ask me anything, okay? That's what I'm here for."

Donna cupped my hand in between hers. "Now, I'd like to arrange sessions with Jaimie to see if we can figure out some roots to Jaimie's struggles. I'll see if I can help bring everyone some peace. Especially to your precious jewel."

I smiled. At least we were on the right path now.

"Will your husband be joining us for the sessions?" she asked, taking out her appointment book.

"No, unfortunately not," I said. "He'd love to participate but he can't take extra time off work. I think he feels more helpless than I do. Jaimie wants nothing to do with her Daddy. He jokes about it but...I can tell he's deeply hurt."

Donna looked at me over her librarian-type glasses. "I'll bring extra information along with me which you can pass along to him then. That way he'll at least feel he's a part of it, okay? Oh! And we'll have to get you to fill out these questionnaires. These will just give us an idea of Jaimie's tolerance level with various sensory activities. The final score will rate the severity of her SPD. You and I can go over the results next time?"

"Thank you," I said.

I just hoped we were doing the right thing.

6 One Step Forward, Two Steps Back...

Donna began weekly visits with Jaimie, who had no interest in this strange woman invading her turf. She made Donna's first few visits very difficult.

When Donna arrived on her first day, Jaimie sat coloring at the kitchen table.

"Hi Jaimie," Donna said. "Is it okay if I sit beside you?" Jaimie nodded, keeping her eyes glued to her paper. She repeatedly drew circles, gripping her crayon so hard that her knuckles turned white.

"Do you want us here or in the living room?" I asked as Jordhan squirmed to be put down.

"You can carry on like usual," Donna said. "It may be good to see how she is with Jordhan here too."

Donna turned her attention back to Jaimie. "Those are some nice circles, Jaimie." Jaimie continued ignoring her.

Donna tried everything she could to get Jaimie to respond to her. With every question Donna asked, Jaimie ground her crayon into her paper even harder. Donna looked at me and nodded—just as she did with the "close to and far from" experiment on her first meeting—then grabbed Jaimie's hand and forced her to draw lines instead. Jaimie froze but she didn't do anything. No screaming, yelling or throwing herself off the chair. She just allowed Donna to move her hand around the paper. Then Jaimie handed Donna a crayon of her own.

"I like circles too, Jaimie," Donna said. "But lines are fun too. See?"

Jaimie looked at the paper where Donna drew her lines then drew circles on top of it.

Donna muffled a giggle. "Okay, let's try something else." She reached into her huge bag of fun and pulled out a bunch of craft items like feathers, pompoms, glue, cut out pieces of paper, and safety scissors. "We're going to make a picture of a turkey that you can show your Daddy."

Jaimie seemed interested in the brightly colored pompoms but when she touched the feathers she pulled her hands back. Donna grabbed Jaimie's hands and forced her to create a picture. Donna wouldn't let Jaimie do anything the way she liked to, causing her to get more and more agitated every passing minute. To make things worse, Donna couldn't understand Jaimie's speech so I had to interpret. Jaimie tried telling Donna she needed to wash her hands.

"Mama, my hands need clean," Jaimie said, her voice trembling.

Donna looked at me with a frown and I told her Jaimie wanted her hands washed. "Not yet, Jaimie. When we're done." the OT said.

"No, *now*," said Jaimie.

"No," Donna said firmly. "Not now. When we're finished."

I chewed the inside of my lip as Jordhan studied Jamie's face; then started whining. "Don't worry," I whispered to Jordhan. "Jaimie's fine."

I knew what Donna was trying to do and I respected it. She wanted to try helping Jaimie to experience different sensations and not be scared of them. It was called Sensory Integration Therapy. I'd read about it in *The Out Of Sync Child* she'd given me on her first visit.

From what I understood, different sensations were supposed to be introduced through play so the child learned to associate "feel good" feelings with the sensation instead of fear. Once that happens, the therapist can then teach the child a better coping tool to deal with the sensation. And sometimes, if the child seemed more resistant, the therapist tried incorporating those sensations into activities the child already enjoyed...to make it easier.

So, since two of Jaimie's favorite activities were drawing and crafting, Donna tried using those activities in her therapy approach. And, even though I knew what Donna was trying to do, and I understood the reasoning behind it, I knew what Jaimie's reaction would be so I tried making things better.

I sat Jordhan on my hip and scooted out to the living room for the wipes so Jaimie's could clean her hands. When we came back Jaimie seemed a bit more relaxed because Donna had allowed her to draw circles on her picture.

"Jaimie, I'm going to talk to your Mom now, okay?" Donna said. Jaimie nodded without looking at her.

Donna turned back to me. "Okay. I've stirred up her little world today. I introduced many things and did tasks using all of her senses. How do you think she's doing right now?"

I looked at Jaimie drawing her circles. "I won't know until later," I said. But I already knew I was in trouble.

"I'm going to call you later on and see how things go, okay?" With that Donna packed up here stuff, said goodbye to Jaimie and left.

Jaimie heard the front door shut and sat still. "She go?" she asked.

"Yes, Donna's gone," I said. "Do you like Donna?"

"NO! I *can't* like her!" Jaimie screeched, throwing her crayons. Jordhan's lip quivered then she let out a muffled cry. Jaimie covered her ears and screamed, "'Top! 'Top it Dordee." Jordhan cried harder. I closed my eyes, took a deep breath, and then left Jaimie screaming in the kitchen to put Jordhan down for a nap.

When I got back down stairs, I found that Jaimie had ripped up the turkey picture, broke every one of her crayons, and laid face down in the middle of the mess crying. When I tried rolling her over to pick her up, she rammed her head into the floor.

I gathered her in my arms. "Jaimie, honey," I said. "You need a rest. I promise this will never happen this way again. Come to Mama."

She turned to me with blood trickling from her nose. She touched me with her head then said, "Okay, Mama."

Jaimie let me clean her face—sporting a nice shiner and fat lip—and put her into her bed. I was livid. I phoned Donna, telling her we needed to change our strategy.

"You need to gain Jaimie's trust." I said. "Look, I don't want to tell you how to do your job. *You're* the expert with this SPD thing. But *I'm* the expert with my daughter and I know what works for her. You can't come in here and take away her routine—it's the only thing that keeps her calm. Isn't there a way to work within her routine and slowly change things as she feels safe? If you don't work more slowly with her, she'll reject you completely then we'll be back where we started."

"Chynna," she said. "I am so sorry. I just got Jaimie's results back from her sensory questionnaire. According to what I see here, Jaimie's form of SPD is quite severe. I would never have jumped right in the way I did if I'd seen these scores first. We'll do things a bit differently next time, okay? I promise we'll reach her."

I was relieved she understood but also quite angry that we'd have to start all over again. Before hanging up, I said: "One thing that upsets Jaimie more than anything is touch. So we have to ask you to remember to use touch with her as a last resort. And don't hug her or ask her for hugs. When she's ready, she may do it on her own but if she feels pressured, she won't want anything to do with you."

"Got it," said Donna. "Thanks for telling me that. I'll remember."

That evening, things weren't any better. Jaimie was out of sorts from the moment she got up from her nap until we put her in bed. She refused to eat her dinner, she threw food at Steve, she shoved Jordhan over twice and yelled right in her face, then she had a complete meltdown while we tried giving her a bath—she cried because the water was too high/warm/ wavy; the tap was dripping; she didn't want her hair washed or brushed and we had to force her to brush her teeth. After getting her out of the tub, kicking and screaming, it took me another 45 minutes just to get her diaper and pajamas on. I was so exhausted that I questioned whether the effort to help her was worth the results.

The tension in the house seemed to elevate once Jaimie started therapy. We knew the situation would get worse before it got better—maybe we just didn't think it could get worse. Steve and I fought more than we talked, which was not normal for us. We were a couple who'd always discussed everything because we'd believed that yelling solved nothing. When things were really testy with Jaimie, no one spoke at all. Nights like I described above were more common than not and it was painful.

Jaimie's SPD diagnosis made us better parents because we understood why she acted the way she did. It wasn't bad behavior causing her to act out—it was her reaction to how her sur-roundings made her feel. We stopped trying to discipline her and, instead, offered her comfort and helped her try to work through the tough times. But Jaimie's needs became our primary focus and we inadvertently paid less attention to other things—like ourselves, individually as well as a couple. And Jordhan was greatly affected by our situation too.

Jordhan didn't even seem upset by Jaimie's behavior anymore except for when Jaimie yelled right in her face. In fact, Jordhan started picking up on some of the things Jaimie was doing: she started throwing things, yelling, and hitting. I knew I had to keep trying with the therapy, even when things were tough.

It ripped us apart at the seams and I wasn't sure how much longer our little family could coast along this way. *Something* had to work.

It just had to.

~~~

The following week, on Jaimie's appointment day, Donna called first to ask Jaimie's permission to visit. Jaimie eased by the time we hung up the phone. Donna was much more cautious: She knocked on the door because the doorbell upset Jaimie; she wore dull colors; talked in a low quiet tone; and let Jaimie choose what she wanted to do.

Donna still worked with Jaimie the entire time, I could tell—slight touches here, occasional questions about feelings, telling Jaimie to say, "Help please." whenever she got frustrated, and flourishing her with praise when she did something right. After a few weeks, Jaimie started trusting Donna and became more receptive to the therapy.

Jaimie responded to Donna in ways she'd never responded to anyone else, including me. Jaimie allowed this woman into her little world and I couldn't help but feel jealous. And maybe even a bit hurt. But the fact that Jaimie responded to someone was, for us, a miracle.

Maybe it was also because we all worked together as a family to make changes, not just making Jaimie change. We got a yoga ball to roll Jaimie on and we each took turns too. We got an air mattress for her to jump on for times she needed to stay on the move and we all laid on it when Jaimie had to do some of her sensory exercises. We set up a little pup tent for her where she put her favorite things—Tigger, her pillow, her favorite book and a little stereo—so she could hide somewhere for alone/quiet time. And we learned different activities Jaimie needed for her "Sensory

Diet" to help her feel the world around her without always being afraid.

As Donna explained it to Steve and I, the Sensory Diet was more than what we tried giving Jaimie to eat. It involved various activities to calm, organize, or alert Jaimie's nervous system so she'd feel safer doing the basic things she should have been doing. Once we began seeing what we had to do for her as a diet—part of her basic needs—it all came naturally and made sense.

Some of our techniques involved: deep pressure massage, joint compressions, stretches, rolling/swaddling her in a blanket, getting her to snuggling/squeeze a foamy chair or body pillow, rocking/swaying her or getting her to rock herself in a rocking chair, tight or loose fitting clothing (depending on sensitivity level), weighted vests, soothing smells (like vanilla or lavender), sucking (straws, lollipops), blowing bubbles, squeeze/stress balls, pulling or pushing heavy objects, eating crunchy foods (apples, Cheerios, popcorn, granola) or just letting her spin or run.

Once we realized that knowing about SPD and understanding it were two different things, we became full participants in therapy. We finally had options to help her. We knew if she was "up" we had to give her activities helping her work through her overstimulation and when she was anxious, we had to do more calming activities. We knew when certain activities were a good choice and when others shouldn't be tried. It could still be confusing, of course, because she was different from one day, one hour, and even one minute to the next. But we at least had options.

Finally!

~~~

After a couple of months, Donna noted that very positive changes bloomed in Jaimie too. "I am so impressed with her eye contact," she said. "It's not long but she looks at me when I talk to her. That's very positive and look at this," Donna pointed to

Jaimie's foot touching her leg, "that would never have happened a few months ago."

Jaimie had finally learned that Donna's presence wasn't harmful and that she could be trusted. Jaimie allowed Donna to enter her world of strict routines, need for repetition, and, most importantly, no physical contact. Jaimie still struggled with eating, toileting, and personal hygiene (mostly teeth brushing, hair brushing, baths, getting dressed, and diaper changes) but we all learned ways to cope. Even with all the positive results, she was still having terrible fits.

"When you leave here, she just has a total meltdown," I explained. "She's particularly bad on the day you leave and she doesn't start to come down until the day before you are coming back. Then it starts all over again."

Donna sighed. "Your little girl is very good at holding it together when she has to. It seems she knows how to act in front of people, and then lets loose once they're gone. It's a compliment to you, as odd as that sounds. She feels safe with you and so feels that she can express her true feelings with you. I sure hope it isn't anything specific I'm doing. We'll have to really pay attention to her triggers so that we can call them when we see them and, hopefully, reduce the severity of her reactions later on."

Jaimie enjoyed Donna's visits, despite her reactions. Perhaps Jaimie felt there was finally another person in her life besides me who understood her and liked her in spite of everything. Donna had patience with Jaimie and helped her express in words what had always been trapped in her mind.

Please, God, I prayed every day. Please allow this to continue.

~~~

December snuck up fast and Donna would be on holidays until the New Year. Jaimie decided she wanted to give Donna a Christmas card. She picked one out of the card box and drew lines *and* circles on it.

Jaimie smiled, showing me her artwork. "I give to Donna today?"

"Yes, you can give it to Donna," I said.

Donna didn't do anything therapeutic with Jaimie for their last visit of the year. She brought over a Water Doodle for Jaimie and Jordhan to try and a Christmas Wreath craft. Suddenly, Jaimie jumped up in her usual animated fashion and ran to the kitchen. We heard her stomp back and she waved Donna's card in her little hand.

"Dis for you, Donna," Jaimie said.

"Oh, my," Donna said. "This is for me? Did you draw this yourself?"

"Yup," said Jaimie, pointing to herself.

"This is beautiful, Jaimie," said Donna, then looked at me. "And what beautiful lines." I nodded and gave her a wink. "Jaimie, I'm going to put this on my desk at work for everyone to see."

Jaimie's big smile lit up her whole face and she let out a little giggle. "Yeah, on you desk."

"Jaimie, I'd really like to give you a hug and kiss for this, can I do that?" Donna asked.

I looked over at Jaimie and her beautiful smile had faded. She sat on the couch, clutching her beanie Tigger, and whispered: "No. No hugs. No kiss. No."

Her head bowed down as her lip quivered. My eyes stung with tears and Jordhan fidgeted in response to Jaimie's facial expression.

"Jaimie, it's okay if you don't want to," Donna said. She tried to keep talking but I ushered her out to the front door.

"I'm really sorry," she said with tears in her eyes. "I thought it would be okay to ask. Things were going so well..."

"I know. It's alright." I said.

"Please call me and let me know if she explodes okay? I can help you through it." I gave a weak smile.

When Jaimie heard the door shut, she wailed. I tried some of the techniques Donna showed me—squeezing her, rubbing her arms and legs, giving her Tigger to hold—but I only made the situation worse. My heart sank as Jaimie threw herself backwards onto the couch and screamed in her familiar coping strategy.

"I can't like it, Mama," she screamed.

"I know, honey," I said. "I know. Mama's here."

Jordhan came over to offer Jaimie her Tigger but Jaimie grabbed it and hit her with it. Jordhan didn't cry but cowered behind me.

"It's okay, Jordy," I said. "Jaimie just doesn't feel well. Here, let's go have a rest."

After putting Jordhan in her bed, I went back down to get Jaimie so she could go to her own bed and release the rest of her pent up anger in privacy.

As I started to close the door, she said, "No, Mama. No leave. Stay with Jaimie." My first instinct was to pick her back up but I knew I couldn't. I had to let her try to calm herself down.

"Mama can't stay with you right now, sweets," I said softly. "But I'll be right downstairs if you need me. You try to calm down and have a rest. Then I'll come get you." I closed the door as she continued screaming for me.

I don't know what made me turn the baby monitor on because I heard her just fine without it. Her screams echoed through the tiny machine and as I heard her head banging on her headboard—which she hadn't done in weeks—I closed my eyes and prayed.

~~~

Jaimie slowly regressed back to how she was even before we'd begun her therapy. Steve and I were devastated. We decided to end the sessions with Donna because they simply weren't helping anymore. Jaimie's reactions to the therapy got so severe that we spent more of her waking hours calming her down.

But before leaving Jaimie's life completely, Donna performed one last miracle for us: she completed a detailed report on Jaimie. In the report, she discussed Jaimie's SPD questionnaire results, the areas in which Jaimie was most affected and what therapy methods she had tried. Things may not have worked out with Donna but her fabulously detailed report helped get us an assessment with one of the best community programs in our city.

The most significant statement in Donna's report was where she said, "…the above mentioned sensory preferences may not be the only factors that influence Jaimie's behavior. Follow-up home visits, phone messages, and consultations with Mom and clinical observations suggest that there may be other influences that contribute to Jaimie's inability to function appropriately within her environment. I concur that further exploration and explanation is essential. Perhaps, then, Jaimie no longer needs to ask if anyone loves her."

God bless Donna and the hard work she did to get Jaimie the help she needed. We'll always be grateful to her for what she did. Thanks to her, and her willingness to listen to us, we got further than we ever would have on our own.

Because of her efforts, we had a place continue with.

7 Chynna's Story:
Loving with a Musical Touch

As you already know, I noticed in the hospital shortly after giving birth to Jaimie that she fussed more when we, or the nurses, held her than when she was left in her crib. The nurses all assured me that most babies fuss when they're picked up at first because they aren't used to the sensations.

"It's normal, if you think about it," one night a nurse said. "Imagine how you'd feel if you were in a nice, safe, quiet place only to be shot out into a loud, bright place with dozens of faces shoved in yours. I think I'd be stressed out too. Just give her some time."

Just give her some time.

Those words became like our theme. Time was all we could give Jaimie, under the circumstances. I wanted to give cuddles, kisses, hugs, and love. I wanted to look into my daughter's beautiful blue eyes and feel her soft skin as I stroked her little cheeks or her strawberry blonde downy hair. But whenever I'd tried doing any of those normal signs of Mommy love, she turned away from me or cried.

Jaimie's extreme aversion to touch has been excruciating for me. I'm sure my pain is no more intense that Steve's—just different. Jaimie has never rejected me completely, as she did with him, so I can't even imagine feeling his pain. But I do understand what it's like to share my body with a baby: to feel her move, to see her restless form on the ultrasound, to hear her heartbeat, and to feel her exit my body as I pushed her into the world. And because of all of that, I understand the pain of having to love my child from a distance.

It's not that she didn't love us; we knew she did. She just wasn't able to express her love the way other kids do. When she was a baby, she let me kiss the top of her head. After a while, that wasn't tolerated anymore. So then I was permitted to kiss or hug one of her stuffed animals who'd give it to her for me. After she turned two, Jaimie hugged by sticking her head out and saying, "Hug." And she only did it if she initiated it. Now, on days where Jaimie's sensitivity isn't too bad, she'll ask for me to hug her. The hardest part, though, is waiting for her to ask because if I initiate it, she'll reject me. So, I learned other ways to help comfort and share loving moments with Jaimie even though we can't touch.

One thing I am so grateful for is my gift of music. I may not have had a relationship with my own mother but she blessed me with many creative gifts, such as music, an appreciation for art and a love for writing. I started playing piano singing in choirs at the age of four and was lucky enough to have a piano around. My grandparents had a gorgeous, black-lacquered baby grand in their living room and Mom had her stand-up Steinway.

Mom was a sought-after piano teacher with an awesome reputation for her singing and other musical abilities. These are her incredible accomplishments that people often forget about because she also suffered with bipolar for which she refused to get treated and coped with it, using alcohol and drugs. It made living with her difficult and scary at times. But the one way you could relate to her was through music.

No matter what state of mind Mom was in, when we sat at the piano and played a duet, or sang together, or even threw a Beatles album on the stereo and reminisced, she seemed calmer. It was as though the music soothed the inner beast which she couldn't tame any other way. And I used it to calm myself and get me through some of the bad times too. That's why I used it with Jaimie too.

Whenever Jaimie woke up from a night fright or she melted down—especially from noise or too much activity—I'd put her Baby Einsteins cassette on—preferably Baby Mozart—or a Beatles CD, and she calmed.

Even now, we use music to dance our sillies out, get rid of bad feelings, or to practice our calming exercises. At least during those times, I felt I was being her Mommy and I was helping her to feel better. I reminded myself of those times when I watched others working with and helping her.

I'll admit it. I had a real problem with accepting outside help at first. It wasn't because I was trying to control everything (as some people thought). It was because she was my daughter and I wanted to be the one to help her. And it hurt that I couldn't. After awhile, I knew if I didn't accept help from others, Jaimie would never thrive. And I couldn't live with that.

So I watched from the sidelines as other people watched her, assessed her, diagnosed her, prodded her mind, and reached her in ways Steve and I were never able to. Those experts—those strangers—came into our home (or we went to their offices) and taught Jaimie how to communicate, express herself, and cope. I watched as they earned her trust and even made her laugh, things we had to work our butts off to receive on a daily basis. I was jealous. And it stabbed me right in the heart every time.

But, bit-by-bit, positive changes in Jaimie's little personality blossomed as she slowly allowed us in too. Perhaps she finally realized that there were other people in her life—besides me, and then Donna—who understood how she felt inside and liked her in spite of it. And maybe she needed to see and feel that for herself before she was willing to let us in.

Most importantly, she saw there were things she was good at and she could do even if SPD lurked somewhere in the background. That's an awesome thing because SPD is often called a "hidden disorder." You can't see what's wrong in a child's little face, or on their bodies, like with other disorders. The only thing that told people something was wrong with Jaimie was her overt behavior and her severe reactions to things. But I wanted people to see her for more than that.

Jaimie was intelligent, talented, creative, and blessed with such a big heart. She simply had to learn how to live in the same environment as the rest of us did—just in her own way.

As she learned more effective coping tools, the rest of us learned too. We learned new definitions of patience, understanding, love, and that there are many ways to look at and handle the same situation. We were also reminded that SPD wasn't entirely who Jaimie was. SPD was only a part of her and that was something that we tried to make others understand too.

Jaimie still has a severe aversion to touch but last year I received the best gift from Jaimie I'd ever, or had ever, received: I crouched down one evening so she could touch my leg with her head but she wrapped her tiny arms around my neck and hugged me—*a real hug*. I was in such shock it took me a few seconds to hug her back. Not only that but as I wrapped my arms around her tiny body, she whispered: "I love you, Mama."

For the first time since she was born, I'd experienced the joy that other Mommies did when their children expressed love. I knew her hugs would be rare and far between but I took it as a sign of good things to come.

Maybe, one day I can get a piano so Jaimie and I can sit and play it together, the same way I did with my mother. The ability to love, to calm, and to touch through music is the one thing Mom gave me to pass on.

And for that, I am so grateful.

8 The Long and Winding Road of Therapy

Of course, Donna didn't leave us empty handed. Her detailed report helped us rip through some red tape and she'd also arranged for us to meet with the head psychiatrist of her organization.

"I'd really like for you to meet with Dr. MacKenzie-Keating," said Donna over the phone after we'd ended the sessions. "She's a strong connection to the preschool programs at the Glenrose. She'd be doing this as a personal favor to me, Chynna, so you guys have to make sure to come."

The Glenrose was a rehabilitation hospital in Edmonton. I'd heard of their preschool programs, which came highly recommended. I didn't feel right about putting Jaimie in such programs for a few reasons. First, they required Jaimie to go into a therapeutic setting three or four days a week, three hours each day. There'd have been several different kinds of therapists working with her and, finally, I wouldn't be allowed to go in with her.

Jaimie was barely able to stand an hour with Donna once a week and I had to be there. How was I supposed to feel good about sticking her in one of those programs at the Glenrose? I envisioned standing on the other side of a two-way mirror as someone tried interacting with Jaimie and I wasn't there to comfort her. I just couldn't do it. The whole thing just seemed so...sterile to me.

I'd heard wonderful success stories from other parents about those programs but I knew in my heart Jaimie needed something that moved slower, seemed warmer, and with people like Donna, with whom Jaimie felt genuineness.

Obviously, I couldn't refuse the option outright. We needed to do whatever was necessary and available to us to help Jaimie, even if it ripped my heart out. But I chose to use the Glenrose as a last resort option: if nothing else we tried worked, we'd have done it. Steve and I decided, in the end, to go to the meeting Donna had set up because we needed the recommendation from the psychiatrist to even have that option. I was nervous about everything we had to do.

The meeting with Dr. MacKenzie-Keating was done around a mild Triage Assessment in which she was participating. A Triage Assessment is when a group of professionals, such as psychiatrists, psychologists, occupational therapists, speech therapists, etc., come together to meet with and assess the needs of, a child. It's usually done with the parents or caregivers present and in a child-friendly environment. There were about four other sets of parents besides us with their children, a speech therapist, a physical therapist, and another occupational therapist aside from Donna.

The room was filled with activities aimed specifically for children with sensory challenges. The only reason I picked up on that was because many of the activities were things Donna had suggested or tried with Jaimie: finger-painting, sandboxes, mini-trampoline, air mattresses, weighted vests, yoga balls, even a coloring station with stickers. Jaimie ran around trying everything while Donna kept her company.

Each expert there looked at Jaimie through different eyes, searching for different things. So we knew each of their diagnoses and recommendations for treatments would also differ significantly from one another:

Psychiatrists: Usually the head of the diagnostic team, they specialize in the prevention, diagnosis, and treatment of mental illness. Their focus is what's wrong with your child and they're usually the ones to give the label (such as ADD, SID, etc.). Because they have a medical degree, they are also able to determine physical problems that can stem from the child's disorder. It also means they can prescribe, or suggest prescribing, any sort of medication which they think may help during treatment and therapy.

Psychologists: a psychologist was the person I figured we'd have seen most often as they specialize in research, counseling, and generally helping people cope with everyday problems. They'd help find the appropriate coping skills to help us and Jaimie live with SPD more effectively. They may even help us work on things like calming techniques and discipline. I thought that person would be the most insightful for us, in some ways, because the non-medicinal tools we'd learn from him or her would be more effective in the long run. This person would help us focus on the things around us, natural things, to help Jaimie.

Social Workers: These people have counseling training and connections to government programs. Maybe this person could direct us to government assistance, if required, and other community programs we qualified for.

Occupational Therapist (OT): From what I read, different OTs specialized in different areas. For example, Donna's areas of specialty were children with sensory sensitivities, including eating, toileting issues, and relating to the environment. But they can also help with speech, communication, and behavioral management. Their training is working on a close, one-to-one basis with a child. They're also, as we found out with Donna, the connection among the other players on the team. They'd help Jaimie slowly and gently learn coping mechanisms by exposing her to different types of sensory information and teaching her how to deal with that stimulation.

Vision and speech therapists, physical therapists, and nutritionists—all mentioned in an earlier chapter—were also available but never approached us. We figured that Jaimie most likely didn't need them. Jaimie's speech wasn't great but she at least tried communicating with us and physical therapists usually work with children who needed muscle tone strengthening, which Jaimie didn't need either. We kept an open mind for any and all options, just in case.

Each available therapist came up to us individually to talk about Jaimie. But it became obvious that she had no speech or physical problems so there wasn't much to discuss. As we waited for Dr. MacKenzie-Keating to come over to us, Steve and I watched Jaimie, trying out all the activities.

"Wow." Steve said. "This is a perfect playground for her."

I nodded, watching her bounce on the mini-trampoline. "I know. It's amazing. I wish our basement was bigger!"

Jaimie ran around trying everything but not sticking with one activity for too long. Donna finally got her settled down at the coloring station and gave her a huge pile of stickers. Jaimie was in heaven. Jordhan planted herself at the sandbox/water table. After about half-an-hour, Dr. MacKenzie-Keating finally came over and introduced herself to us.

She sat on the extra toddler chair in front of us. After polite introductions and handshakes, she said, "I've read Jaimie's file and Donna has told me a lot about her." She said, looking over at Jaimie and Donna. "It's good that Donna could be here for her today."

I smiled. "Yeah. Donna is a familiar face. Jaimie liked her a lot."

"But you ended the sessions with Donna, correct?" Dr. Keating said, leaning in closer to me. "Donna mentioned Jaimie had tremendous difficulty with coming down and preparing for the sessions."

We discussed the steps Donna took before coming over and how terrible Jaimie's fits were during the week after her visits.

"Jaimie's reactions got too severe." I said. "We were devastated because we hoped this would've helped—and it did for awhile—but something about the sessions or Donna upset Jaimie too much and she took it out on the rest of us."

Dr. Keating then asked us a few questions about our family history with mental illness, or if anyone else in either of our families was autistic, or had sensory issues. We covered my pregnancy and Jaimie's birth. Then we briefly talked about what sorts of coping methods we'd used.

With every question we answered, I felt more and more like we were under a microscope. Many of the questions Dr. Keating asked us, Donna had already asked but the ones about our family histories, the type of relationship each of us shared with Jaimie, as well as what coping methods each of us used with her, were new and intimidating.

She must have sensed my discomfort. She touched my knee and said, "I'm just trying to get a feel for what you guys are going through so we know what direction to send you in."

I was taking my psychology degree. I knew how the counseling routine went. She asked questions, we answered them, and then she repeated what we said with a tag on like, "Is that right?" I felt like saying, "Look, Dr., cut the crap and let's get to it. We know what we go through in our house. We know what Jaimie has and we've researched it fully. You've got a file on her an inch thick on your lap full of reports, assessment results, and diagnostic reports. Enough is enough. Tell us what to do for her!"

Instead, I clutched my hands together and took a deep breath. I answered her seemingly endless questions as completely as I could; told her the methods we'd tried and were trying, what worked and what didn't. Poor Steve just sat there, barely saying a word. I hoped at the very least we'd be able to help him learn how he could be a daddy to his daughter. I so wanted that for him.

Dr. Keating highly recommended the Glenrose programs—of course, since she headed a couple of them!—and told us trying to get Jaimie into some sort of playgroup with other children her age would be a great thing for her.

"Donna was right when she said you need to get her out more, even if she struggles." the doctor said. "Jaimie is a bright girl who seems interested in her surroundings but struggles to interact with it because of her sensory issues. We need to get her out there practicing the skills Donna and you two have been teaching her or she'll never be comfortable. Donna will call you with a few playgroups you can try or see what you can find on your own. I highly recommend ones involving movement, music and crafting as those are her areas of strength."

Finally, she made a recommendation to get Jaimie into a local community program called CASA (Child and Adolescent Services Association) for long-term assistance. Essentially, CASA provided the same sort of support and assistance we'd been receiving all along with the same sorts of professionals (psychiatrists, psychologists etc.) The difference was that CASA provided assistance to children, youth, and families until they were 18. That was what we were looking for.

The program Jaimie was in at the time, the one Donna was a part of, ended when Jaimie turned three and that wasn't too far away from the meeting with Dr. Keating. If we hadn't found a path to follow soon after then, we'd have been stuck on our own.

In the end, I promised to look into playgroups for Jaimie and we consented to have Jaimie put on a waiting list with the Glenrose as well as to have the recommendation put through to CASA. I found the entire process rather intimidating. It was almost as though they made all the decisions for us and we were just going along for the ride, giving our consent when necessary. I didn't like it.

I wasn't a control-freak—I knew when it was best to let others handle something. But I also knew Jaimie better than anyone and nobody seemed to recognize that the times Jaimie responded the best to treatment or therapy was when it worked within her comfort zones instead of forcing her to do what others thought was best.

Plus, from what I'd heard from other parents, as well as my own research, what really worried me about CASA, and the Glenrose programs, was that they were very supportive of medicinal therapies. That was something both Steve and I were against for a child as young as Jaimie was at the time. But we didn't say anything.

All we did at that point was wait for phone calls from either place when Jaimie's name came up on the arm's length waiting list. Until then, all we could do was conduct more research on our own, be strong about the sort of treatment we wanted for our daughter, and pray.

~~~

Jaimie's third birthday came and went. We still didn't have her in any sort of therapy nor did I find a suitable playgroup for her. But we weren't left completely on our own because we were still connected to the EEIP and their resources. Maria came for follow-up visits every few weeks to see how we were doing. Just before the time Jaimie had to be released from the program, Maria set up a meeting for me with the head coordinator of the EEIP, Joan MacDonald.

"I think you may find a meeting with Joan very useful," Maria said. "She has a teenage daughter with SPD. Perhaps she can give you some insight, encouragement, or support that I can't give you on this subject."

I knew why the idea for the meeting came about. I'd been procrastinating on getting Jaimie into a play program. A lot of the places, which Donna suggested, were for children with developmental delays. And even though Jaimie had a diagnosis of SPD, she had no speech delays, no physical impairments, no hearing problems, or other such disabilities. Her only struggle was her severe sensory issues and the anxiety that stemmed from those issues. Her seemingly normal functioning in the other developmental areas disqualified her from certain play programs. But when I'd tried out—and I don't like using this word—"normal" play programs, Jaimie wasn't able to participate with the "normal" children and I'd end up pulling her out. It was as if we were stuck in the middle between what was considered "disabled" and what was considered "functioning well."

I needed insight from an expert—a person who'd been where I was. So, I agreed to meet with Joan, who came to my home with Maria the following week. Joan was like a breath of fresh air. Finally I had a person who sat with me and said, "I know what you mean." and truly knew.

In the past, I'd found a few online support groups but Steve and I never knew anyone near us with a child like Jaimie or who understood what it was like. Therefore, I welcomed Joan with open arms.

Joan's daughter also had SPD and Joan went through hell on earth to get her daughter the proper treatment—just like our story. Like Jaimie, her daughter was able to function well on most other levels but her sensory issues prevented her from joining activities or participating socially the way she wanted to. As well, her daughter went through a lot of the same assessments Jaimie was going to have to and she did it at a much older age (Joan's daughter was in her early teens during most of her assessments.)

As Jaimie jumped around from one couch to the other, speaking rapidly, Joan smiled. "Wow, I cannot believe how much she's like my daughter was at this age. It's amazing."

We talked about Jaimie's file, her progress, and our mutual respect for Donna.

"Donna is an amazing person and a fantastic occupational therapist," Joan said. "I'm glad she was able to give you some direction. I'm just sorry she wasn't able to reach Jaimie the way she wanted to. I know she wished she could have done more."

"She did a lot," I said. "Even now."

The main reason for Joan's visit was to help arm me with information for our Triage Assessment with CASA. I had no idea what was involved and was scared. Well, we had insight about what happened from the psychologist's view but I wanted to know what it was like from a person who'd gone through it— especially what it was like for the child.

"Well," Joan started. "My daughter was a lot older than Jaimie when she went in for an assessment. So, the experts interacted with her directly while I sat with her. For Jaimie, you'd most likely go into a room filled with toys and activities so Jaimie and Jordhan can play while you're free to talk with the psychologist. They'll probably have an OT there to help out with the girls too, if needed."

She said there'd be a two-way mirror where another group of experts would observe the interview. Usually this group included another psychologist, psychiatrist, speech and/or physical therapist, physician and others, depending on the needs of the child. For Jaimie, there was to be the head psychiatrist, another OT and some sort of child behavioral expert. On top of all of that, the session would be taped for later review, evaluation and diagnosis.

"One thing you should also know about CASA is that they are strong supporters of medicinal treatment." Joan added. "In fact, it's usually one of the first things they recommend in the more difficult cases. It may be recommended for Jaimie because of her severe reactions to things, her anxiety, and her inability to calm herself. But never be afraid to say what you do and don't want. Don't be bullied into anything."

Steve and I already knew drug therapy would be presented as an option. It wasn't to say we'd never consider drugs if Jaimie needed them later on down the road. But we felt there had to be better options out there—more holistic options—for a three-year old child. And we stuck with that decision.

The visit with Joan proved comforting as well as insightful. Not only were we given advice and tips for handling the assessments, I was also given a glimpse into Jaimie's future through Joan's daughter. At the time we met, her daughter was 15 years old. She was taking anti-anxiety medication but she functioned well as long as she was given enough preparation for new situations or upcoming events and also given appropriate calm-down time after such events. She did great in school and had several friends. She even participated in a few social activities.

It was tremendously encouraging and I needed to hear all of that. I needed to see that everything we'd been going through was worth it. I needed to know that the assessments, the examinations, and the meetings would amount to something some day. I needed to hear that the coping tools and mechanisms we were learning would be helpful to Jaimie down the road. And, most of all, I wanted proof that all the crap we'd gone through was helping, even though we couldn't see it then.

Before leaving, Joan said, "Don't give up, Chynna. You've come so far and done so much. Things will be okay." And she hugged me.

After that meeting, my strength recharged. The determination I'd had in the beginning when trying to get people to listen to us returned. And the best way I thought I could help Jaimie while waiting for phone calls was through "field research."

In order to understand my daughter's world, and how the therapy was supposed to help her, I needed to live in her world *her way*. I needed to feel how things felt to her, smell how things smelled to her and see things through her eyes. So, shortly before starting at CASA, I did some "field research." I wore the itchiest wool sweaters or other irritating fabrics right on my skin and tried concentrating on tasks at hand; I wore my shoes on the wrong feet and tried carrying on regular physical activities; I shined a bright lamp in my face while trying to do homework or writing; I spent a couple of days doing everything with my left hand instead of my right; I put on my winter clothes in the middle of the summer then tried doing my daily routine; I drank water with loads of salt in it or ate extremely spicy foods or eating next to kitchen window after they'd mowed the lawn or before the garbage truck emptied the garbage bin out in the parking lot (WOW! That was awful!).

These may have seemed like extreme things to do—and some of them were—but until I did those things I had no sense of what or how Jaimie felt. After I did my field research, I had much more patience with her reactions to things, people, and situations and was able to spot triggers before they had a chance to affect her adversely. That didn't mean I could change everything but I was at least able to warn her that such-and-such was going to happen which would feel/smell/look like this-or-that and we could do something to help her through it. It made me feel closer to Jaimie and it bonded us in a way we hadn't been able to if I hadn't done those things.

With my mental notes from my own personal research, and Joan's wisdom, I was ready for whatever came next. It gave me hope and I was more determined than ever to get Jaimie what she needed to live her life.

~~~

The next several months, while waiting for CASA to call us, proved to be the most stressful. Jaimie wasn't receiving any sort of therapy and she struggled more than ever. She needed to have the bars put back on her bed; her night frights intensified; she refused to leave the house; and her eating and toileting difficulties worsened. What made matters worse was that Steve and I were so frustrated with what was going on around us, we started taking it out on each other.

He called me during his lunch hour asking whether I'd called one place or heard back from another. "No, I haven't," I said icily. "And, like I told you yesterday—and the last time you asked—there's nothing I can do. We're on a list. I can't exactly get us bumped up on the list. We just have to wait."

"I just need to know we're on the track to something," he said. "I feel helpless enough not being able to physically help her. The least I can do is help get the show on the go. I have to see something's getting done, or will be getting done. It's ridiculous."

I understood, of course. There's nothing worse than being told you're "on the waiting list" with nothing more you can do than to wait. It is frustrating. But what was I supposed to do? Rush in the place like Rambo demanding to be heard? We needed to be patient, which was really hard for me.

We finally received our phone call that Jaimie was next on the list and our appointment was set up with instructions for our Triage Assessment. We were more than prepared.

For Jaimie, all we could do was tell her we were going to another school to play. For us, we read our instruction sheets, all of the material provided to us by EEIP and my journals I'd kept over the years. We were armed and as ready as we could be. Of course, no amount of preparation sets you up for the actual day.

On our Triage day, we waited for someone to collect us from the waiting room. Jaimie and Jordhan played with a few toys and Steve and I sat in hard metal chairs holding hands. Then a man came around the glass wall and introduced himself. "Steve and Chynna? I'm Brian. I'm the psychologist who'll be heading our interview."

We all shook hands, said our pleasantries, talked about the lovely spring weather, and then sauntered down to the interview rooms. Jaimie wouldn't let me hold her hand but she clutched her beanie Tigger so hard her knuckles turned white. I ran my fingers down the length of her hair and she tilted her head into my palm.

At the end of the hallway, a small group of people were there, waiting for us. We were introduced to the head psychiatrist of CASA's preschool programs, a couple of OTs, a speech therapist, and a couple of psychology students. More handshakes, more pleasantries, and then the psychiatrist explained what would happen.

"Steve and Chynna, you will be going into this room of fun over here with your beautiful daughters and Brian," she said. "The rest of us will be in this room here. We will be observing all you through a two-way mirror and the session will be recorded. Try to relax and take your time. We aren't here to judge. My only focus is Jaimie. I will be watching how she interacts with everyone and everything around her. Karen here will join you to assist with the girls, if necessary. At the end, I will join you to discuss our observations and what we'll be doing from here. Any questions before we begin?"

We both shook our heads. Jaimie refused to go into the room at first. But once she saw all the toys and books, she tiptoed through the doorway, gripping Tigger's neck in her fist.

"Wow," said Brian. "Someone sure has a tight grip on Tigger!"

I smiled. "He's her best friend and confidante."

Jaimie hid her face with Tigger and followed Jordhan to the toy shelf. The rest of us sat in the chairs on the opposite side of the room. Brian whipped out a pad of paper and our file.

"Okay," he said. "Now I know you've answered many of these questions—probably a few times—but we need to start from the beginning in order to have everything in our file too. Please bear with me."

He started with our family histories: our childhoods, our relationships with our parents and siblings (past and present), health histories, mental health histories, and our feelings toward

our families. I fought tears the entire time. To be fair, though, I
was more emotional than usual for two reasons: My mother had
passed away the day before our meeting and I'd just found out
that we were going to have another baby.

My mother and I weren't very close but her death still hurt.
And I knew they'd be asking us questions about our family
histories. I knew their interest in our families only had to do with
any patterns of Jaimie's disorder or if our family had any interactions with her, which they didn't since they were all in other
provinces. Steve and I had nothing to hide. But it was still rather
difficult answering certain questions and it wasn't easy being the
receivers of a question firing squad. It was much more intense
than the question session with Dr. Keating.

Steve didn't, and never did have, a close relationship with his
father and when asked about him he said, "We had no emotional
relationship at all and we don't communicate now. I know the
way he handled problems and feelings has a lot to do with how
I'm dealing with things. We just weren't supposed to talk about
stuff like that, you know. Guys just don't."

But Steve was very close to his mother and I to my Uncle
Craig, stepmother, and siblings. So we showed that, despite a few
negative relationships, we did have positive, loving ones too.
(Note: I found out later that they'd asked about such things to
confirm that Jaimie's problems were more neurological and not
mental or emotional. The latter are easier to acknowledge,
diagnose, and treat.)

From there we moved to my pregnancy and birth with Jaimie;
then into the nitty-gritty about when we'd first noticed her
behavior. I think the most difficult question for either of us to
answer was, "How would you describe your relationship with
Jaimie?"

I answered first. "Close," I said. "She trusts me with everything. With me, she never has to worry that things won't be done
wrong because I've learned what sets her off; what she needs to

stay calm; how to get her to listen; or even what she'll eat. She still has fits with me but she'll at least let me get close enough to sing to her or do her deep-touch stuff to calm her. But, at the same time, it's also a heart-breaking relationship because I can't love her the way a Mommy is supposed to love their child. It hurts."

Then Brian asked Steve the same question. Steve said, "Jaimie and I have no relationship at all. She won't let me touch her, talk to her, or even do anything for her. And if I do, she gets worse."

"So you've been fathering your child from a distance then, Steve," Brian said.

"Yeah, I guess you can say that," Steve said. "With Jordy, I can hold her and tell her that I love her and stuff. It wasn't until we had her that I felt like a Dad. I want to help Jaimie; I just don't know how I can."

I reached out and grabbed Steve's arm. "It's been so hard for him to watch from the sidelines. With Jordhan, he's a very hands-on Daddy. I'm so grateful that he's at least gotten to experience that with her. But I'd still love for him to find a way to experience some connection with Jaimie. And for her to find some way to connect with him. It's too hard this way."

Brian nodded while he wrote. "That's exactly what we hope to do."

The interview went on for over two and a half hours. Jaimie was at the end of her rope. Near the end, I had to find Jaimie a coloring book and crayons. She turned her back to all of us and rocked while she colored. I had to end the interview after that.

The psychiatrist came into the room right after I said we needed to go. Right off the bat, she assured us that, in her opinion, Jaimie wasn't autistic but that she definitely had severe sensory issues. She also felt Jaimie had other issues they needed to explore more before an official diagnosis could be made.

"Jaimie seems bright, intelligent, and very interested in her surroundings. I noted many times where she walked up to items or toys and stared at them but chose something else. She didn't make eye contact or interact with anyone but did keep her eye on Chynna the entire time. I also noted her extreme discomfort with transition and with people trying to interact with or touch her."

It was such a relief to hear someone else saying they saw what we did without us having to prompt them. Jaimie was going to start something called Play Therapy with Brian the following week. What worked for us was there was no talk about drugs—at least not then—and they promised to work within Jaimie's comfort zones.

Of course, they still wouldn't give a solid diagnosis beyond her SPD but words like Obsessive-Compulsive Disorder (OCD) and high anxiety were tossed around. We had to do more questionnaires, more assessments, and Jaimie would have to meet more professionals. I didn't like it but at least things were finally moving forward.

I just hoped they kept going in that direction.

9	# HELP!

"Play Therapy is based upon the fact that play is the child's natural medium of self-expression. It is an opportunity which is given to the child to 'play out' his feelings and problems just as, in certain types of adult therapy, an individual 'talks out' his difficulties."

—Virginia Axline

Jaimie was just over three when she began her sessions with Brian. I prayed night and day that it ended up being our breakthrough therapy to reach into Jaimie's world. It was our last step before having to consent to more aggressive therapy through the Glenrose because everything else we'd tried until then had failed. And Steve was getting anxious.

Steve and I loved our children, and each other, very much. But when it came to Jaimie, we saw things completely differently. I felt, and what had usually worked with me, that the slow and steady approach was the best approach in dealing with Jaimie. I found if you went too quickly with her or didn't take the time to work something new into her existing routine, things backfired. Steve wasn't completely sold on my view.

He accepted the slow and steady view but thought we that needed to take a much stronger stand with her. "If we coddle her for too long, she'll never be brave enough to move forward," he kept saying. "We need to take a stand now, while she's young, because it's only going to get harder the older she gets."

I knew he had a point. But with all the failures we'd had up to that point, I didn't want to put her through any more assessments, reviews, new people or places. I just couldn't do it. Each time she'd fallen down, it took her even longer to get back up again and it hurt to go through it with her. So, we agreed that if play therapy didn't work, I'd agree to give consent to the preschool program at the Glenrose. And, at first, I thought it was going to go Steve's way.

Jaimie hated going to therapy at first. I had to prepare her for three days in advance before her therapy day. It was always a catch-22, preparing her for everything. We did it so she wouldn't worry as much but she did anyway. But if we didn't prepare her, the aftermath would be twice as bad. I learned from the experiences with Donna: always prepare Jaimie as much as humanly possible in advance of upcoming events.

Brian was very helpful by making Jaimie's appointments on the same days. But the entire process started on Friday. At naptime, I'd say something like, "We're going to the school to see Brian on Monday, Jaimie. Won't that be fun?"

"Tomorrow?" she asked. She didn't know the days of the week. But each day had a specific thing we routinely did so she'd remember.

"No," I said. "Tomorrow we go to the drug store, the meat store and McDonald's for lunch, remember?"

Then there'd be much discussion about how Daddy would drive us to CASA, that we'd take the cab home, have a picnic snack while we waited for it, etc. But she needed to discuss the entire process several times over and over. Then her night frights would be awful the few nights before and the night of, as well as the night after, her appointment. I was always asked why we put ourselves through the agony of pre-warning her about events but, honestly, it was much worse if we didn't remind her or if, God forbid, we surprised her with something.

Obviously we couldn't prepare her for everything but when we couldn't, she'd completely shut down and became even more rigid with her routine. So, we just lived with the excess…excessiveness for a few days. It was better than the alternative. And the routine was even worse when people came to visit.

It was worse whenever we had visitors—even her beloved Grams—because people came onto her turf messing with her routine. Even if Jaimie was genuinely excited for the visit, like she was whenever Grams came up, it was still difficult for her to get through. We had to start at least a week before Grams came, explain that, "Grams comes on a plane and Daddy picks her up. Then she'll come visit us for a bit until bath time when Daddy will take her to her hotel."

We'd have to go through the same process at the beginning of each day Grams was there because Jaimie had to prepare before Grams came over. Even though she loved her Grams, Jaimie couldn't deal with the extra person around. Then just as she got used to Grams' presence, she'd have to say goodbye and get used to her not coming over. It was draining.

But even with the best preparation, Jaimie still struggled. For the first several therapy sessions, Jaimie absorbed herself in the play with her back turned to the rest of us and never responded. Brian said it didn't matter because she was working through things even if she wasn't talking to us. I didn't get it. How was this stupid therapy helping her if she was able to act the same way there that she did at home?

Sensing our frustration, Brian asked if he could tape the sessions so he could play it back for us near the end to go over the strengths and weaknesses. "Sure, why not!" we said. By then we were used to being observed, taped and recorded. Boy, what an eye-opener that was.

We were able to see how, even though Jaimie didn't talk to us directly, she was attempting to include us in her play. In one scene, Jaimie played with kitchen stuff and pretend food. She made tea and said under her breath, "I think I'll have some tea. I've had enough coffee this morning." Steve says that almost every morning he's at home. Then she shoved a tiny plastic cup at him.

"Thank you," Steve said. "I hope it's Green Tea. That's my favorite."

"Green Tea. Yeah." Jaimie said, smiling.

I was floored. I must have missed that exchange while I played with Jordhan. That was the most verbal communication Jaimie and Steve ever had that didn't involve screaming, yelling, and crying...*ever*. I mean, she didn't look at him or talk to him anymore than that but it was such a wonderful thing to see.

I looked at Steve. "See? I told you this would work if we were patient. She included you in her playing!"

Steve smiled.

"Steve," said Brian. "That was an excellent exchange. Did you see how her total stance changed when you showed interest in what she was doing without asking a question? That's exactly what you do in free play. Great job!"

It was a positive step in the right direction. *A breakthrough.* For the first time since she was born, Jaimie tried to find a way to reach out to Steve. She still didn't allow him to do anything for her and got extremely agitated even at the thought of him caring for her on his own, but she tried to let him in.

The Play Therapy route proved to be the most valuable tool we'd come across. Things at home were somewhat more peaceful. Jaimie's night terrors were reduced to one or two per week, her fits weren't lasting as long, her sensitivity to everything didn't seem quite as bad and, most importantly, she used play to communicate with us. All we had to do was sit near her when she'd be playing and she'd either hand us something to play with her or she'd talk to us through her toys. It was wonderful. But, sadly, after a few months Jaimie seemed to regress again.

One morning, I took her and Jordhan to the park by our house. We were there for about twenty minutes when the children from a local daycare flooded the park. A little girl came over to introduce herself to Jaimie, who was digging a hole in the sand. After a few minutes of the little girl trying to get Jaimie talking, Jaimie screamed and ran off into the field. That wasn't the first time she'd done something like that but I was so hoping it wouldn't happen again for a long time.

The poor little girl looked at me with tears in her eyes. "I'm sorry." she said.

I touched her cheek and said: "Don't worry. You didn't do anything wrong. Jaimie just isn't used to other kids. Thank you for trying."

Then I grabbed Jordhan, carrying her like a football and speed-walked after Jaimie. (Not an easy task at six months pregnant!) She never ran too far away. Only far enough to get away from what scared her but still close enough that I could still see her. That didn't mean she'd make it easy for me to get her home, though.

"C'mon Jaimie, honey," I said. "I know something upset you at the park. Why don't we go home and talk about it."

She sat in the grass, hugging herself. "No."

I knelt beside her with Jordhan hugging my side. "Can you tell me what happened? Or what we need to do to make you feel better."

She flew herself backward into the tall grass. "No."

I could have cried. What was I supposed to do?—sit in the dry, itchy grass for hours until she felt like talking to me. Then Jordhan had a suggestion: "Spin."

Jaimie stared at the clouds. I watched Jordhan from the corner of my eye as she got up, spread her arms out, and twirled around. Jaimie didn't move for at first. Then she got up and spun with

Jordhan. What a smart girl Jordhan was—not quite two, but knowing what things made Jaimie feel better enough to talk.

The girls spun for a while. It didn't even matter that mosquitoes were snacking on us; only that Jaimie calmed down. Both girls crumbled into heaps on the grass as they laughed. Things almost seemed normal.

"I need to go down the twisty yellow slide, Mama. That girl stopped me." Jaimie said out of nowhere.

Jaimie had a routine at the park: swings, hole digging, go down all the slides once, and then go home for snack. The girl interrupted her.

"Go. Then we'll go home for snack," I said. Jordhan and I watched Jaimie run to the slide. When she came back, it was like nothing happened. She felt better. This was wrong and so unfair. There was no way Jaimie's obsessiveness with her routine, or her reaction to having it interrupted, had anything to do with her SPD. And when I talked to Steve about what had happened later on, he was livid. And he let Brian know.

"Okay, we've been coming here for several months now and what we've learned has really helped us at home, especially with me and Jaimie," he said. "But we've got to get moving here. Jaimie is getting worse again, she's turning four soon and we can't put her into a class with other kids when she's like this. We need some direction; a plan. I don't want my daughter to get further behind than she already is."

Steve is a man who never talked much unless you asked him something, or if he was really angry. And when it came to his kids, don't mess with him. It was great to have him be the one handling the reins for a change. And Brian seemed to listen to Steve better than he did to me.

We were set up for a meeting with the head psychiatrist for a review of Jaimie's file and to see what further options we had. Like Steve said, Brian had given us so many important tools to work with Jaimie and play therapy was such a blessing. But it simply wasn't enough. Jaimie needed more because even though she was better on some levels (coping), she was the same or worse on others (sensory, tantrums, social interaction, etc.) And Brian wasn't able to give us any further options or direction. We needed a higher source.

I was so nervous about that meeting for several reasons, but mainly because: (a) I knew Jaimie would leave there with even more labels that she already had, and (b) I had a feeling that drug therapy would be given as an option. But we wanted to talk to the "Head Cheese" because she was who'd be able to get us through the red tape we faced. We'd patiently put our time in for months to be able to meet with the psychiatrist. Jaimie needed her help.

The meeting was conducted in the doctor's office—a room very similar to the therapy rooms only a bit neater and more organized. One side of the office was tailored to the younger patients: mini kitchen set, table and chairs, toys, stuffed animals, and puppets. The other side was more office-like with her desk, meeting chairs, and shelves stuffed full of therapy books. The lollipop tree on the corner of her desk—basically a Styrofoam tree with suckers sticking out of it—was a reminder of the Dr.'s softer side (and believe me, we needed that reminder several times throughout our interview.)

We filed into the small room and were ushered into seats beside the psychiatrist's desk.

"I hope you don't mind," she said over her glasses. "We have an intern with us today."

It didn't make any difference at that point. We were all getting used to telling our story to different faces, or groups, at a time. She'd obviously reviewed Jaimie's file, which grew to over two inches at that point, before our arrival because we barely had to give her any information on our history.

"What are your primary concerns with little Jaimie?" she said.

I looked back at Steve who seemed as confused by the question as I was. Surely if she'd read the file, or had been briefed by Brian on a monthly basis, she'd already known what our primary concerns were.

I spoke first. "Well...uhm...mainly we're most concerned with all of the things concerning everyday living like her bathroom issues, her eating problems, her social issues, and her sleeping problems. We're used to her sensory stuff and her fits. Those seem to change from day to day based on the other things. We figure if we can help her with those other areas, her fits and stuff may go down. Hopefully. That's why we're here—to see what we can do."

Steve nodded. "We just want to get going in a solid direction because things are starting to stand still again. We're tired of putting her in things that don't work."

Actually, at that time, Jaimie's toileting issues were the highest concern. Yes, she restricted her foods because of textures but the girl held her poop for several days at a time. We tried putting her on the potty or toilet but you can't make a kid poop if they don't want to! It was so bad at times that if we'd gotten to three or four days in a row—worse than when she'd been a bit younger—without her pooping, we had to give her a suppository and, believe me, it took several hours to days before she got over that. Her doctor ended up putting her on laculose (an orange-colored sugary syrup) that softened the stools enough where the person can't hold it in. Because the dose her pediatrician put her on wasn't working; the psychiatrist increased the dose and its amount.

She also gave us another questionnaire based on anxiety. Essentially, we learned from the two-hour meeting was that on top of her SPD, Jaimie had General Anxiety, Separation Anxiety, severe Social Anxiety, and Obsessive Compulsive Disorder. The Doctor said that Jaimie's anxiety most likely stemmed from her 'D issues and her inability to cope with it effectively. Then she reached into her desk and pulled out a yellow pamphlet on anti-anxiety/anti-depression medication—SSRIs.

"I know you don't want to treat Jaimie with medication," she said. "But I wouldn't rule it out completely. If Jaimie is dealing with all of this anxiety on top of her sensory issues, it's no wonder none of her prior treatment is effective. The medication may help calm her enough to be able to concentrate on her treatment."

She then turned to her intern to explain why she said what she did and to discuss the medication. Steve's jaw clenched so tightly I thought it would pop out.

"Excuse me," he said. "I don't mean to interrupt but what the hell are we supposed to do with all of this?"

The doctor frowned. "What do you mean, Steve?"

"I mean you give us all of these labels and tell us to put her on drugs." he said. "That's not a solution to me. A three-year old kid doesn't need drugs. I can go to our next-door neighbor and buy drugs. We came here for some guidance...a solution."

"We made it quite clear we won't consider drugs for Jaimie." I said. "At least not at this age. Surely there's got to be a more holistic way to treat her at this stage."

The psychiatrist leaned forward. "Yes, there's diet, the play you do with Brian, there are some preschool programs at the Glenrose that I head. There are other approaches but all we're saying is don't rule out medication. If it's something she needs later on, be open-minded to the idea. Okay?"

We gave consent to have a community outreach program contact us. We were frustrated. It was the same thing as always: consent, waiting list, patience, failure. Maybe we weren't pushing hard enough; maybe we weren't making ourselves clear enough; maybe Jaimie needed to have an all-out throw-down meltdown for anyone to totally understand. We stuck it out with CASA for about six more months, and then tapered off our therapy. We didn't want to cut ourselves completely off from CASA because they were an awesome connection to other programs. But it just wasn't helping. In fact, it was only making things worse.

~~~

We had one more meeting with Jaimie's therapy team when her fits worsened again. The second meeting was much more relaxed and so was the doctor—perhaps, because there was no intern observing her. Either way, our concerns were still the same and we still refused any medicinal treatment. That time, she gave us a few more options.

"First of all, let's help poor Jaimie with her elimination difficulties," she said. "I understand her fussiness with eating and that most likely isn't helping this situation. I'm going to give you a few recipes for treats—or what she'll think are treats—that are actually extremely high in fiber. That will be a start."

She then gave us a few pointers in helping introduce foods into her diet while still respecting her high textural sensitivities. "Why don't we have an additional place mat for her or bowl at the table so that she can put the foods in her mouth, give them a try, then have the option of spitting it out if it feels too much for her. At the very least, she can taste these foods and may even surprise herself by liking them when she isn't too sensitive."

I didn't mind the idea but Steve didn't want Jaimie getting into the habit of being able to spit out her food. With Jaimie, we'd always had to be careful what we introduce because she worked things into her routine and once there, it's even more difficult to change it. But it was an option.

"Now, we have to find a way to help Jaimie cope with her anxiety so she'll let herself sleep. You've said that her sensory symptoms are much worse when she's tired, correct?"

We nodded.

"What we need to do is introduce some quieter activities before bath and bedtime, which you two have done a wonderful job at maintaining for her. Let's start reading more books, or doing some quiet time listening to music, or even getting her to be in her tent before bath. No wrestling, Dad, okay? No running around, no crazy activities."

Steve repressed a laugh after she winked at him. "Now, Chynna, let's try and talk to Jaimie and work more on getting her to use her words. And we have to use the advice Brian is giving you about helping her associate words with her feelings. She has extremely strong verbal skills. Let's use that to teach her to connect to herself and to us."

Her greatest concern seemed to be with getting Jaimie into preschool. "We need to find some sort of program to get Jaimie into. If you want, I can put to get her into one of the Glenrose programs but she may not qualify for most of them anymore, mostly due to her age. Keep in contact with Brian about options. I'll bet that many people guess Jaimie's age incorrectly because of her height. And when they find out her real age, their expectations are higher, because they don't understand her special needs. The way I see it, if we don't get her into a program soon, she'll never feel comfortable enough to be around other children."

Actually, she knew Jaimie would technically be supposed to start kindergarten in the fall, but didn't even feel she'd be able to handle preschool. Even Jaimie's pediatrician told us that if we weren't more aggressive in getting Jaimie help, she'd never be at the same social level as her peers. He also told us not to turn our backs on Jaimie's psychiatrist as she was an invaluable resource. We knew that. And we were trying to take advantage of that resource.

After that meeting, a letter on our behalf to a place called Community Options where Jaimie was supposed to obtain assistance with school as well as to receive some sort of assistance at home. We got our copy of their letter, which she warned us would be an absolute worst case scenario in order to get Jaimie help, then we waited. And waited. And waited.

In fact, Jaimie went through an entire preschool year without ever hearing back from any of Jaimie's therapists or Community

Options. And when I called them for myself to find out what was going on, we were told that Jaimie was on a waiting list. Again.

I was told that because Jaimie didn't have any other disabilities or difficulties, she may not qualify for assistance in school or anywhere else. Jaimie had strong verbal skills, was eager to learn new things, and had average fine and gross motor skills. All that was really "wrong" with her was her SPD and the anxieties that she's also been diagnosed with.

Apparently, Jaimie wasn't considered disabled enough for assistance even though we struggled most of the time just to get her dressed or go to the bathroom or even get her to eat or dressed. Jaimie didn't even have the skills to function normally with kids her own age or cope with normal sensory stimulation the way other people could but nobody felt she had enough of a problem to need assistance. Or that we needed help to be proper parents to her!

I realized that if we wanted to get anywhere in helping Jaimie, we'd have to be more aggressive, more assertive, and even greater advocates. Not only did we have to inform people what SPD was and how to help Jaimie function in their world, we also had to fight just to get her into the same programs as her peers.

Jaimie fought on her own far too long. That was it. I decided to use every resource and talent I had to do what we needed to do. I was going to be the voice Jaimie didn't have and people were going to listen.

No matter what!

10 | Babies, Brain Food, Jenna, and Fun Factory: Our Holistic Approach

After the last meeting with the psychiatrist, I started researching nutritional options. Honestly, because Jaimie ate so little as it was, I was a bit nervous messing with her eating. But we'd committed to more holistic, natural therapies for Jaimie so I knew something needed to be done. One thing to change was creating a "brain-friendly" diet for Jaimie.

Because SPD is a neurological disorder, it was important to make sure Jaimie got a lot of healthy brain food, including "good" fats such as Omega-3. Of course, all children needed healthy brain foods but, as I found out, it's essential for children with SPD for three important reasons:

(1) The brain is 60% fat. If we don't give the brain healthy fats, it'll get it anyway it can and that's when we turn to the naughty saturated fats. Children with neurological disorders, such as Autism and SPD, are susceptible to becoming junk-food junkies because their brains crave fat but they don't choose the best ones;

(2) Many children with SPD have a tendency to avoid many foods due to their sensitive senses regarding smell and texture. This can lead to missing the crucial vitamins, minerals, and fats, which their tiny brains need to cope with their symptoms. Learning how to

sneak those brain foods into their fussy diets is a bonus; and

(3) Nutritionists who specialize in SPD and sensory sensitive children have discussed how making simple but important changes to the diet can dramatically reduce sensory symptoms.

Bearing all these in mind, the following were the most important foods that I was told to include into Jaimie's overall sensory integration diet:

(1) Oily fish such as wild salmon, mackerel, and tuna are all packed with DHA (docosahexanoic acid—try to say that five times!), which is one of the best forms of Omega-3.

(2) Nuts, especially almonds, are a great source of fats, vitamins (B and E), and minerals (magnesium) and, apparently, excellent for the brain's grey matter. In layman's terms, grey matter is an essential component of the central nervous system, which helps in the routing of sensory and motor messages throughout the body. The main target of SPD is the nervous system, particularly the autonomic system. So get those children nutty about nuts (if there's no allergy, of course.)

(3) Berries like blueberries and strawberries contain antioxidants and help with coordination, memory, and cognition. Sneak these luscious berries in a smoothie with some flax seed oil for a tasty brain-powered snack!

(4) Veggies containing antioxidants like the vitamins C and E, such as bell peppers and broccoli. Yes, even children without sensory sensitivities protest broccoli but try it with cheese or healthy dips!

(5) Yogurt contains tyrosine, which is known to give you a little pick up and increase mental awareness. Try Greek

yogurt to avoid the extra sugar found in the flavored sorts. You can always add a child's favorite fruit for some extra flavor.

(6) Beans are an excellent source of B vitamins and fiber. Mashed up, they can be a great addition to sauces, dips, and soups.

(7) Flax seeds and oil are a fantastic source of Omega-3. The seeds would need some getting-used-to but the oil can be mixed in with muffins, cookies, smoothies, and other treats.

(8) "Smart" oils like walnut, flax seed, olive, and avocado are all excellent sources of Omega-3. Cook with them; make salad dressings or dips with them. They all have a stronger taste, however, and a child with a more sensitive palate may need to get used to them.

(9) Eggs contain a nutrient called choline. To get a bit technical, choline is needed to create acetylcholine, which is good for memory. Jaimie doesn't like the texture of eggs but we add Omega-3 rich eggs to her muffins, pancakes, and baking treats.

(10) Tempeh is a fermented soybean cake similar to tofu. Yes, it sounds gross and you'll definitely have to disguise it in other things but it is such an awesome source of protein and B_{12}. The great thing about it is it absorbs the flavor of whatever you cook it with; so try adding it to stews, soups, or stir-fry.

Aside from the fact that we were a household with both nut and fish allergies, the most challenging thing had been coaxing Jaimie into trying anything new. Her palate was so sensitive that she'd actually thrown up right at the table simply because something didn't feel right on her tongue. Her diet, for the longest time, consisted of plain pasta, green apples, and plain bagels. As time went on—much, much later in her therapy—we'd gotten her to try muffins (that I'd "brain-ified" with flax seed oil), homemade pasta sauce (which I'd shredded veggies into), chicken and, even pizza—all of which we'd tweaked one way or another. At that point, I considered any meal where Jaimie tried even just a lick of something new a huge success. But it wasn't just Jaimie's eating that needed more attention and changing. There were other problems we'd been ignoring.

Even though SPD was Jaimie's disorder, the rest of us were greatly impacted by certain aspects of it. Most specifically was how isolated we'd all become.

There were days when leaving the sanctity of our house was too much for Jaimie. When things were a real struggle for her, she wasn't able to handle a light breeze on her skin or the wind blowing her hair or even how bright the sun was. On days like that, I wouldn't even be able to get her to go out on our front lawn, never mind going out on a more exciting adventure.

There was nothing wrong with staying inside once in a while but there seemed to be more days inside—in the safety and familiarity of our house—than those outside. And I understood her need to stay close to home when she didn't feel brave enough to venture out. But I worried about poor Jordhan.

At two, Jordhan's verbal skills weren't off to a great start and she was painfully shy. How was she supposed to practice being around other people when she wasn't exposed to them as much as she should have been?

Another thing was, and I feel horrible even thinking about it now, that Jordhan thought all kids were like Jaimie. She was scared to talk with, get close to, make noise around, or play with other children, and I knew something had to be done about that. It wasn't fair to keep her cooped up in our house all the time just because Jaimie wasn't able to cope with things on a certain day. And I understood how she felt—even I felt the need to be around other people.

Plus with the new baby due in the fall, it would be a lot harder to get out and about. I wanted to get out and have fun with my girls while it was still easier to get around. But just as I'd found an appropriate playgroup for us, Jaimie had another setback.

It got to the point where I couldn't even force her outside even to take the cab to see Brian. One morning, prior to one of our last sessions before the summer, I phoned to cancel our appointment because Jaimie refused to leave the house. He counseled me over the phone.

"Perhaps we've been pushing her too far too fast," he suggested. "We've been trying to prepare her for the baby, she'll be starting her pre-preschool class; she knows our sessions will be ending for a few months…we don't think of it but these are all very large transitions for Jaimie."

I didn't answer.

"On days, such as today, where she may not be brave enough to venture any further than the front yard, that's just fine," he continued. "We'll just give her a lot of praise so, maybe, she'll be brave enough to go a bit further the next day. You already know there'll be a step or two forward then two or more back in these early years. Just hang in there."

My chest tightened as he went on. I wasn't angry necessarily with him, but more at the situation itself. It happened every time: things would be going great and then, once Jaimie resisted the treatment or regressed, the therapist didn't know what to do. In fact, they started telling us to do things we'd already been trying as though they didn't know what happened and were giving up. It must have been so hard for Jaimie.

Jaimie did her best but none of her counselors or therapists— except maybe Donna—ever tried seeing things through her eyes. I only imagined how difficult it must have been for her not to be able to express exactly what she wanted and/or needed in a way others could understand.

·d with that was that those people she couldn't
:ate with tried teaching her how to communicate using
 ‗‗ ‗at she didn't feel comfortable using. In fact, even when
Jaimie tried expressing herself, she was told it "wasn't the right
way." Then those people tried making Jaimie do things their
way—their "right way"—without trying variations of their way
to see what worked best. Finally, how she related to those people
changed on a daily basis, depending on her own sensitivity levels.
If she wasn't able to deal with a person's smell, for example, she
wasn't able to concentrate on the task at hand, which caused
frustration on both sides.

How difficult it must be trying to reach a child like that and,
my God, how hard it must be on the child. That child was my
Jaimie and somehow I had to educate those other people so everyone could understand what she was going through. And it wasn't
the everyday people or teachers or neighbors or friends and
family that I had trouble making understand Jaimie's needs—it
was those people trying to reach her.

I didn't want to come across as a pushy, over-bearing mom.
Jaimie wasn't a child you could just grab and make do things. She
didn't learn by punishment or regular forms of hard-handed
discipline. You couldn't yell at her or guilt her into doing things.
The reason she broke down so much, and so severely, was
because she was so smart. She knew how to do things, how to
speak, what to say…it just didn't come for her as easily. It made
her angry. And if those professionals got frustrated with her, she
felt even worse about herself and she'd shut down.

I saw it time and again. And I wished I could find someone
who'd try understanding her more and having patience with her
while still allowing her to be who she was underneath it all—a
beautiful, smart little girl.

~~~

Since Play Therapy wasn't working for Jaimie any longer, I
needed to find other options. I bought book after book, stayed up

night after night researching different sorts of therapies (and there are some whoppers out there!) and also reached out to the lovely parents in my SPD support groups.

I never realized how many different directions we could go in. The focus was usually on helping the child involved cope with their sensory issues while giving the parents tips on how to help the coping process along. Here are a few of the more common approaches suggested to me:

Home Visits: A therapist, usually an OT or a psychologist, comes into the home to give therapeutic sessions. With some children, who find more clinical environments more stressful, this form of therapy is perfect. It also has the advantage of having techniques learned in the child's natural environment so it may be easier for him to both learn the skills as well as to accept them into their routine. The disadvantage, at least in our case, is that the child isn't always able to separate therapy from his safe place (home) and this can cause him even more anxiety.

Clinical Therapy Sessions: As opposed to the home visits, the advantage is that the child can go out for their therapy then be able to go back to their safe place to "let down." Plus it gives the child practice with going out into the "real world" and having to cope with other people in other environments. If the sessions are worked into the child's routine, he or she may be more accepting to it. A disadvantage is that some children may find it hard to generalize what they've learned in the therapeutic session into their home environment.

Group Therapy: This form of treatment uses the same techniques used in individual therapy sessions but integrated with drawing from other people for additional support. For younger children, it is set up almost like a preschool setting. This form of therapy works best with children who have no issues being with or playing with other children. For severe SPD, or children with autism, this form may be too much for them to handle at first.

But it's important as it teaches the child how to get along with other people.

Hospital Preschool Intervention: Here in Edmonton, an excellent program is called "1-2-3 Go!" and is conducted through the Glenrose Rehabilitation Hospital. To qualify for this program, the child must have, "complex needs due to neuromotor, neurodevelopmental and/or neurobehavioral disorders requiring intensive, specialized early intervention service or further diagnostic treatment." Jaimie qualified for this program but we wanted to try a less intense and clinical setting before having to resort to it. As excellent a program as it is, the focus is on treating the child and the parents aren't allowed to be in the room during sessions. The parent watches from a two-way mirror while their child, along with a handful of other children, is interacting with psychologists, OT, speech therapists, or other professionals.

For me, this proved so difficult, especially if Jaimie "lost it" and I wasn't allowed to go to her. But, in some more severe cases, it may be the only option.

Play Therapy: This is one of the most raved about and non-intrusive ways to treat a child's behavioral difficulties. Essentially what happens is that the child engages in non-directive play while their therapist simply observes: how they interact with the toy/object; what they're saying during play; how long they're able to engage in play with the toy/object, etc. All the therapist does is throw in a supportive interjection every so often to let the child know someone is still there.

The idea is to help the child use the toys as a way to deal with feelings they can't express in any other way. The hope is that once they can draw these feelings out through play, they'll eventually feel they can share their feelings with the therapist or family in a more productive way. Jaimie was enrolled in this form of treatment and it helped us so much.

Physical Therapy: These therapists help to improve a person's physical ability. For children with SPD, they encourage activities that help to strengthen muscular control and motor coordination so the child can prepare his or her muscles for movement.

Speech Therapy: This form of therapy helps children learn to strengthen their speech skills. Children are also helped with strengthening their oral-motor control which can help in other areas such as eating.

Visual and Auditory Training: Being able to see is one thing; being able to determine what one sees is another. A lot of children with SPD have difficulty with fine-motor coordination, hand control and visual discrimination. All of these things are determined by how they see things. That's what visual therapy helps with. Hearing not only helps children communicate better but also incorporated into gross motor skills, balance, posture, and body awareness. Auditory therapy will help children in these areas and it will also help teach them how to discriminate and/or attend to different noises.

Jaimie, similar to a lot of other children with SPD, has great difficulty with "tuning things out" and being able to focus on a task at hand. Children like these benefit greatly from these therapies as it can help both at home and in school.

Nutritional Therapy: Conducted by a nutritionist and helps children and their families maintain optimum health through the combination of carbohydrates, fats, protein, vitamins, minerals, and water.

Sensory Integration Therapy (Sensory Diet): As Carol Stock Kranowitz stated in her book, there are three questions parents should ask themselves while figuring out whether they need to seek a diagnosis of SPD: (1) Does their child's struggles get in their way?; (2) Does their child's struggles get in other people's way?; and (3) Should the parents listen when others, such as teachers, pediatricians, or friends and family, suggest to seek additional help?

The Sensory Diet isn't another special food diet, although changing nutritional needs would be something considered. It's a combination of tactics and methods, individualized to the child, used to help teach a child with SPD learn how to relate to his or her environment in safer, more effective ways. A great example would be Jaimie's need to spin, run, and jump. Obviously, such things would interfere in a regular classroom but if we give her a safe time and place to do so, she's able to relieve some of her anxiety.

Carol Stock Kranowitz suggests the following in helping parents create a successful Sensory Diet program specialized to their child's needs. First, set up specific times to perform the activities. Then try to supply the activity the child needs or wants. But, of course, you have to be realistic...Jaimie loves to bounce on the couches but that's neither safe nor something I want the other three children in our house to do. So, we found an inflatable trampoline we set up in the basement for her. Now she can jump no matter what it's like outside!

Next, children need to be able to direct the sort of play they need/want. If they need stimulation, find safe, sensory-stimulating activities (such as running in a field, lifting heavy things, or jumping on a mini-trampoline. There are even aerobics out there for youngsters.

Also try changing the routine and environment occasionally. Yes, change is very difficult for these children but they have to expect the unexpected once in a while if he or she expects to get along in the world around them.

Most importantly, parents need to be in tune with their child's needs and be certain the home is a "sensory nutritious" place for their child. If not, find somewhere to take them. It's okay...really! And in some situations, especially for Jaimie, it is better that they find things outside of the house that provide the therapeutic aspect so they can come home to the safe place for their serenity.

Some of those we'd tried already to that point; others we
to wait until she was older. But since our main focus was fir
a more holistic natural approach for Jaimie, I also checked into
therapeutic approaches not usually discussed—especially not by
those in the medical field. Here are a few of them:

(a) **Chiropractic:** I would never have thought to use this
approach with children but considering that the focus of
chiropractics is to address abnormal movement of our nerves,
muscles, and joints, it seems a logical choice. It helps with posture
and teaches the child to be more aware of their movements in
their environments.

(b) **Craniosacral Therapy (CST):** This is something I'd never
heard of until I joined a SPD parent support group. Basically
someone assesses how well the child's craniosacral system works.
That's a confusing word that just means they check to see the
effectiveness of the membranes and fluid that helps to protect the
brain and spine. All that's done is light touch massage on the
bones and structures of the skull. It's supposed to help correct the
adverse results (such as sensory, motor, and neurological
dysfunction) stemming from imbalances during the development
of the brain and spinal cord. Carol Stock Kranowitz recommends
checking out Dr. John Upledger's website at www.upledger.com
for more information. The few parents I'd spoken with on this
therapy seemed pleased with the results.

(c) **Hippotherapy:** This is another form of therapy I learned
about through my SPD parent support group. It's supposed to
help posture, movement, and sensory processing. Essentially, OTs
and physical and speech therapists integrate movements of horses
into regular therapy interventions. One mother in my group said
it did wonders for her son's muscle tone, reaction to stimulation,
and sensory-motor skills. Who knew?

(d) **Perceptual Motor Therapy:** Donna used a form of this with
Jaimie to help her with fine motor and visual discrimination. The
idea is to get the child to participate in activities stimulating

left/right brain integration so he, or she, learns to be more in tune with what's happening to the nervous system when they do things.

The last forms of therapy mentioned may sound a little out there, but like other parents of SPD children, I'm even willing to delve into the little or unknown to help Jaimie learn to live her life without pain or fear.

It's all for the greater good.

~~~

Just before the summer in 2006, close to when Jaimie's therapy ended for the summer, I registered Jaimie in a pre-preschool class called, "My First Preschool," at our local YMCA. It was perfect for Jaimie.

It was only an hour long with fifteen minutes of free play at the beginning, then a craft, followed by story time, and some singing and dancing to wrap up the hour. Those were all her favorite activities that we did at home so I thought she'd have a blast! Plus the class size was small (about 10 other children), Jordhan was allowed to join her, and I could stay with her too. But Jaimie just wasn't ready.

She was confused about what to do in the free play. She needed structure and routine; so when we walked into the classroom, and she didn't know where to go or how to start, she broke down right away. She loved the rest of the class, so I knew if I could get her past the first 15 minutes, we'd be okay. Then her teacher made a fatal error one day by grabbing Jaimie by her arms and saying, (too sternly, in my opinion), "Jaimie, you must wash your hands like everyone else. Get over there."

I knew we had to teach Jaimie that, eventually, she'd need to follow the rules of the teacher at hand. Not all teachers would allow her just to use her anti-septic foam and wipes because she hated the feeling of the water and/or soap on her hands. And they wouldn't understand her aversion to such things either, no matter how much I tried explaining it to them. I also empathized with how irritating it must have been to have a child who wasn't willing to go along with the others and you didn't understand why. But, geez, ask me!

I found the teacher's reaction disturbing, actually. I gave her information about SPD and a sheet of Jaimie's history, including a brief description of her triggers. I even emphasized that the teacher, and any of her helpers, should consider touch as a last resort. And not once did I intervene when the teacher tried guiding, teaching, or helping Jaimie. I couldn't believe it. Because of that one outburst, Jaimie refused to go into any more classes with that teacher and I had to pull the girls out. Boy, did I ever get flack for that decision!

I realized my choice wasn't the way to show them to mow through adversity and keep trying. And, perhaps, I was more emotional than usual, being pregnant, but it was painful watching Jaimie sit in the corner of the room with her hands over her ears crying while all the other children in the group were having fun, including Jordhan.

All I wanted to do was show Jaimie it was okay to make friends, that other kids will like her as much as Jordhan and I did. But she wouldn't (or couldn't) allow herself to try. I knew, then, that I needed to find another way to make Jaimie feel good about making friends. Maybe in a safer environment.

A few days later, Steve and I took the girls for a walk around our neighborhood. A new couple moved into the townhouse across from us. They were a beautiful young couple with a little girl about Jordhan's age so we wanted to take the girls over to introduce them. I thought even if Jaimie was too scared to meet or play with the little girl, Jordhan may warm up to the idea. Wouldn't it have been fabulous to have a little friend so close? I was too nervous to go over at first because I wasn't sure how Jaimie would react. So, I let the girls lead the way.

We walked by the couple's house pulling the girls in their wagon. Suddenly, this gorgeous little red-haired girl bounded up to us and tried getting in with them.

"Jenna!" her Dad said. "That's not your wagon. I'm so sorry. She really wants one of those. She's been eyeballing yours every time you guys go for a ride."

We all laughed. "No worries," I said. "Anytime she'd like to join us for a spin, she's more than welcome."

We introduced ourselves. As we made small talk about the weather, what we all did for work and where we moved from, I heard Jaimie laughing. It was a beautiful sound we didn't hear often and this huge-hearted Jenna brought it out in Jaimie.

All three girls sat in the wagon—Jenna sitting in the middle— and chatting away as though they'd been friends for years. There was no crying, screaming, or yelling. Jaimie didn't run away or even try moving away from Jenna. And at the end of our little visit Jaimie allowed Jenna to hug her. I almost cried.

Jenna was Jaimie's first little friend. Yes, she was younger but they were all basically at the same level, socially. And the fact that Jaimie sought out a playmate was a miracle to us. Jenna's friendship meant--and still means—the world to Jaimie and it has given her the courage to be around other children. I don't think those lovely people will ever know how much they've meant to us but I knew we were meant to meet up.

We spent the summer having playmates, pool parties, and Care Bear tea parties at each other's places. Things went so well Jaimie and Jordhan were invited to Jenna's birthday party in September. We told Melissa and Jason (Jenna's parents) about Jaimie's SPD. Even though there'd only be a handful of times Jaimie had broken down, when she played with Jenna, we explained things to them because Jaimie's reactions scared Jenna at first. But after awhile, and because they understood her, if or when Jaimie melted down, when we were with them, it was no big deal. Even with their love and understanding, I was still nervous about a birthday party.

We'd always downplayed Jaimie's birthdays. The hustle and bustle of birthday parties had been too much for her in the past. In fact, she cried just when we sang "Happy Birthday" to her. But she seemed genuinely excited about going to Jenna's house for a party. It was in a safe environment that she was both familiar with and comfortable in. So we figured what the heck! We lived right across the street so that if something did happen, and Jaimie needed her quiet place, we could just walk back home. And Melissa, as always, was willing to help make things a bit more tolerable for Jaimie:

"Why don't you guys come over a bit earlier," she said. "We know you guys have an earlier routine than us and the girls can all play together before everyone else arrives. It may be easier for Jaimie too."

When we first arrived, Jaimie sat on their couch and zoned out. That was our way to describe whenever Jaimie sat in a quiet place, tuned us all out, and was unresponsive. When she'd first started to do that, we worried something more serious was wrong. But eventually we figured out it was her way of calming herself down whenever she was in new situations or with new people. She sat that way for a good five or ten minutes, then jumped off the couch, and joined the Jenna and Jordhan.

She made it through the whole party without any fits or crying. It took a long time to calm her down afterwards, and she didn't sleep that night, but she did it. We were so proud of her. It was the first of many baby-steps and it was good experiences like that that helped us through her setbacks.

A few weeks later, Jenna invited the girls to go Trick-or-Treating with her. Jaimie was interested in the prospect of getting candy but not about having to either wear a costume or go up to strangers' houses asking for treats. But she said she wanted to give it a try that year. That marked the first Halloween ever Jaimie showed any interest in.

It certainly helped that Jenna's favorite holiday was Halloween—her excitement was contagious. Again Jaimie surprised me with her enthusiasm. It was snowing and icy on Halloween night that year and we had to cut our candy adventure short due to slipping on the ice but, again, she did it! Whatever insecurities or fears she had were eased whenever Jenna joined her in something new. I remember thinking, "It's too bad we can't bring Jenna everywhere with us...or clone her, somehow."

Even the arrival of Xander, our new baby boy, that November wasn't as hard on Jaimie as we thought it would be. She still had a problem with me being in the hospital for a couple of nights and away from her. And she still wouldn't let Steve do anything for her. But she learned something even more exciting: that she could do some things on her own. For me that was a phenomenal achievement because Xander turned out to be a very fussy baby and I wasn't always able to jump to Jaimie's demands when she needed something done.

It wasn't that Jaimie was a demanding child. She got used to me doing everything for her because (a) she made herself believe she couldn't do things and (b) she'd always been afraid of how things would make her feel. When she started doing things for herself, she sprouted some self-confidence she'd never had before. It was such a relief to tell her, "You can do it, Jaimie!" and have her respond with, "I know, Mama!"

Things were going so well that we started prepping Jaimie for regular preschool in the next fall before her fifth birthday. We kept her back a year in order to give her a bit more exposure to different people and situations so the next time she was in a classroom she'd be more receptive to the idea. We decided to give the preschool program at the YMCA, called "Fun Factory," a try. We also decided that two days a week would be a perfect way to ease Jaimie into the school idea.

After our struggles with the pre-preschool classes at the YMCA, I was admittedly very nervous about putting Jaimie into a regular preschool class. But a meeting with Karen, the head of preschool programs, put me at ease.

I'm sure I came across as neurotic at the beginning of our conversation. "This just has to work," I said, speaking faster than I usually do. "This will be our third try putting Jaimie in a preschool program and I just want to set her up for success. I can't let her stay at home hiding from the world anymore. All I want for her is happiness and to experience life as fully as she can. I know she can't enjoy it exactly the same way we all do but if we tweak things for her just a bit, maybe she'll try."

Karen touched my shoulder then said, "Let's tweak then. What can we do?"

For the first time since Donna, I had someone who was willing to work with me to help Jaimie. Karen never told us what she thought was best nor tried to change her. Instead, she used what Jaimie was good at and comfortable with, and then went from there. In fact, she tweaked the environment to suit Jaimie's needs and not the other way around. I knew I'd made the right choice.

All summer long, we prepared Jaimie for her first day of school. We visited the YMCA and showed her where her class would be. Closer to the day, we went on the actual school days to form the routine. When we received the welcome sheets, I told Jaimie what she'd be doing in her class. And the week before classes, Karen set up a meeting for Jaimie to meet her teachers, Kennedy and Judith. She wouldn't speak to either of them or eye contact but, at the very least, she didn't try hiding her face or standing behind me.

It sounded like a lot of work but the more time spent in getting Jaimie ready for that huge event, the more likely she'd accept going and, maybe, enjoying it. And I was willing to do anything in my power in helping to make this ride less bumpy for her. I was not going to let what happened last time happen again.

On the first day of preschool, Jaimie seemed genuinely excited. Steve stayed with Xander out in the hallway while I went into the room with Jaimie and Jordhan. Each of them chose a storage box for their shoes and snacks; then we followed the other children through the door. Jordhan ran over to play with some blocks but Jaimie shoved her head into my thighs and cried, "Don't leave me, Mama."

Because there were several children doing the same thing—typical for all preschoolers on the first day of school—we didn't draw attention to ourselves too much. In fact, during our conversation, Karen called the first month of preschool "The Months of Tears." The difference was that I wasn't able to calm Jaimie. She wanted me there but when I tried comforting her, she screamed, "Don't touch me, Mama." For a split second, I thought of removing her. Instead, I guided her over to the book area they'd set up for her with her head still securely wedged in my thighs. I knelt down on the mini ABC rug and Jaimie lay on the floor, not moving her face from my lap.

I tried everything I could think of to get her to respond to me. Nothing worked. I stayed strong. I had to make her do it. She needed to make herself do it. I fought back tears when Judith, the head preschool teacher, came offering her assistance.

She crouched down, put her hand on my shoulder, and said, "Hi Jaimie," she said. "Remember me? We met a few weeks ago."

No response. Jaimie wedged her face deeper into my legs.

Judith tried again. "I'd really love to play with you, Jaimie. We'll have a lot of fun!"

Nothing.

"We have crayons or PlayDoh," she said. "I remember your Mama saying you liked those things. Would you like to start there with me?"

That sparked a bit of interest. Jaimie turned her head sideways, shoving Soodee securely into her nose, then looked in Judith's direction. "I don't like the smell in here," Jaimie said. "And the lights are too shiny."

Judith smiled, and then whispered to Jaimie. "I know what you mean about the lights, Jaimie. They give me a headache sometimes. Why don't we try to do something so we can tune them out? Would you like to try?"

Jaimie glanced over at the PlayDoh table. "Only if Mama stays too."

I didn't say a word. Judith said, "Of course, Mama can stay for a little while but you know she'll have to go. We only let kids stay in here. No grown-ups allowed except for Teacher Kennedy and myself."

Judith stuck her hand out to guide Jaimie to the station but Jaimie shoved her hands under her tummy. "No," she said. "No hands."

Judith slapped her forehead. "Oh gosh, Jaimie. I forgot about that. No worries. You come on your own, okay? I'll meet you over there."

I waited. When Jaimie hadn't moved in about five minutes, I decided to remove her. Tears stung my eyes again as I reached across her body to lift her up. *We'll just try again another day*, I thought. Suddenly, Jaimie stood up, grabbed my hand and walked us over to the PlayDoh table.

"Hi Jaimie," Judith said. "I'm so happy you decided to join us. We have pink today. You like pink?"

Jaimie nodded. It was another half-an hour before she felt comfortable enough for me to leave but we did it! Once she got into her PlayDoh creation, I slipped out and I watched her through the window for a while. Jaimie went back over to the book section several times but she stayed for the entire class, right by Jordhan's side. I cried. Fortunately, there were other teary-deary Moms around whom I blended in with.

Good for you, my girl.

By December, Jaimie was used to the routine and knew what to expect when she got into class. For some reason, she still experienced tremendous stress with the Free Play part of preschool, so the teachers and I came up with an idea. There were still stations set up but the teachers always had at least one station set up with one of Jaimie's favorite activities, such as PlayDoh, coloring or stickers. That way, she always had a place of familiarity to start with so that she felt more confident venturing into other stations. That seemed to help quite a bit.

The amount of time I had to stay with Jaimie before she'd let me leave lessened until I was able to say, "Okay, Jaimie. One station change then we'll do 'high-fives' and I'll go."

She still didn't pay attention to the other children, even when they'd go right up and ask her to play with them. She played beside the other children instead of with them, except Jordy. But Jordy wasn't always patient with Jaimie's desperate need to stay close. She finally got a taste of what it was like to socialize with kids her own age and wanted to make her own friends aside from Jaimie. That seemed to hurt Jaimie tremendously. Still, Jaimie made some fantastic progress despite her anxiety.

The biggest step she took was participating in Show-and-Share. I watched from the window as Jaimie stepped in front of her little classmates and proudly held up her Funshine Bear. My heart filled with joy. She even answered their questions. My little Jaimie who, a few months earlier, wasn't brave enough to walk out our front door, stood in front of her class and joined them in fun. I was so glad I had Kleenex with me that day!

During all of those new changes, Steve and I found out that I was pregnant with our fourth—and last—child. We chose not to tell Jaimie or anyone else about it until things were smoother for Jaimie in school, or until I couldn't hide it anymore. Besides, I didn't even want to think about having another baby with everything else that was going on. Our lives were already so busy. But, like always, God had a plan for things happening the way they did.

By March 2008, things changed again. Judith wasn't in the classroom anymore and neither was Kennedy. Jaimie took a real shining to Kennedy too. Kennedy never once made Jaimie feel like a "special needs child." She focused on Jaimie's strengths, and accepted her the way she was. But that spring, Jaimie's beloved Teacher Kennedy was promoted to a different position within the YMCA and was no longer in the classroom. That was difficult enough for Jaimie. The worst part came after Kennedy left; there was a cycle of different substitute teachers. It seemed like every week we went to class, there was a new face teaching the students. That's difficult for any child but for one with a need for routine, and a fear of new people and situations, it was too much for Jaimie.

Some days, I fought with Jaimie just to get her into the cab to go to the school. On days when the teacher of the day was a person Jaimie couldn't relate to, she ran to the waiting area and hid under the tables. A few times, Kennedy was kind enough to come to our side of the building to help coax Jaimie back out and into the classroom. She'd even stayed with Jaimie until she felt better. Naturally, Jaimie's behavior near the end of her school year caused great concern for Steve and me. If she wasn't able to handle the dynamics of the preschool classroom, how on earth was she going to handle the curriculum of a regular school in kindergarten?

On a more promising note, Jaimie's teachers told me that she "Has a tremendous desire and eagerness to learn. She puts her hand up to answer questions, she pays attention to our lessons--as long as she's put up front, or on the edge of the circle—she asks for help when she needs it, and asks questions."

Those, we thought, were all very important skills to have. And we hoped they'd be the base for helping Jaimie to get through the next phase in her little life.

Teaching Teachers, and Other Grown-Ups, How To Teach

We realized that, perhaps, a great deal of Jaimie's problems near the end of her preschool year were that she was more stressed and worried than usual...about me.

During a routine ultrasound, ironically around the same time that Jaimie had too many changes in her preschool classroom, we were told that the baby I carried had a heart abnormality: the structures on the right side of her heart measured larger than normal and she had a thickening in her aorta valve. Yet again, no one was able to tell us how the abnormality would affect our new baby, or even if it would. Even top pediatric cardiologists weren't able to give us a solid diagnosis until after the baby was born. So, for two and a half months, we had to "relax" and "not worry" as thoughts of the worst flooded our brains anyway.

Here Jaimie needed me more than ever and I had to prepare myself for the horrific possibility of saying goodbye to a baby we'd never met. I tried my best never to show my worry in front of Jaimie because she fed on other people's stress, especially mine. But Jaimie was a smart girl.

Even at five-years old, she was able to pick up on the fact that something was wrong when Mama had to keep going into the hospital for "tummy movies", when my OB/GYN made a big deal of the baby's heartbeat and I was in and out of the emergency for the last few weeks, mostly due to false labor that my own stress put me into.

Fortunately, Jaimie had gone through pregnancy with us twice previously, so she knew that, one day, she'd have to be with Daddy while I was in the hospital with the baby. This time was very different, though. At one appointment, my OB/GYN made the mistake of telling us that the baby would have to go into the Neonatal Intensive Care Unit (NICU) right after she was born.

Jaimie's face frowned and teared up. "You mean, baby Sophie isn't going to come home with us, Mama? Where will she go? Won't she be lonely?"

Jaimie found out we were having another girl and she was so excited. She even helped me pick out her name. But as soon as all the heart-monitoring appointments began, and Jaimie feared something was going to happen to the baby, she stuck to me like glue. Whenever I sat on the couch for a rest, she laid beside me with her head on my tummy. She always talked to my tummy and rubbed it so the baby heard her—and my tummy stretched and kicked in response to her voice. And she had to be with me at every appointment, no matter what it was. I think she worried that something bad was going to happen to me too. And it affected every area of her life.

That's when her behavior deteriorated at school and she refused to go. She didn't want to leave me, or baby Sophie, for one second. She got up every hour at night to make sure I was still there. And God forbid she woke up when I was in the shower or somewhere else in the house and she only saw Steve when she came downstairs! It was horrible. Once again, I wasn't able to enjoy the baby inside of me because the one outside of me needed me so much more. And even though I was terrified of what was to happen with our new baby, I worried more about Jaimie.

Trying to find more proactive and positive ways to distract myself, I decided to focus on what I could do. I couldn't control what was going on with the baby, nor had any control over what would happen to her, but I was able to help Jaimie prepare for Kindergarten. Now, I won't lie—if the decision about Jaimie's education had been entirely mine, I would've chosen to home school her. In my opinion, if what surrounded Jaimie upset her so much that it distracted her from learning, teaching her at home combined with enrolling her in a lot of extracurricular activities so she'd still have that social contact, gave her a fighting chance. Steve didn't agree with me.

He agreed with Jaimie's therapists who felt that for a girl like Jaimie, who feared the outside world so much, allowing her to stay at home even more often only encouraged her social fears. So I agreed, reluctantly, to give public school a chance—with a warning: "We'll try this until after Grade one," I said. "If we find that her social anxieties are the same, or get worse, I'll educate her at home."

Steve didn't agree but he didn't disagree either. "We have to do everything else that's available to help her *before* trying that route. I just don't think letting her stay home is the answer. Let's keep it a safe place but not her recluse."

We researched several schools in our area before finally deciding on one which was perfect for several reasons. First, the school was right across the field from our home so no more cabs. Plus, Jaimie knew the school was close to home so I hoped that would reduce some anxiety and worrying. Second, there was a preschool room down the hall from the kindergarten room so Jordy would be in the school a few days a week too. Third, the school was well-connected with local community programs, such as PUF and Community Options, which helped special needs children integrate with their peers. The bonus above all of that was that Jaimie would have a top-notch Kindergarten teacher in her corner.

"Mrs. P." as she told her students to call her, was supposed to have retired the year before Jaimie started. She kept agreeing to stay on specifically for children with high needs that tended to get lost in the education system shuffle.

"I have a soft spot in my heart for these kids," Mrs. P. said during one of our lengthy telephone conversations. "If teachers don't fight for them now and give them the initial tools they need to forge ahead, what will happen to them later on?"

Many parents of special needs children sought out Mrs. P. because of her many decades of experience, her concrete solid connections to various assistance programs in the city as well as her gentle and encouraging approach to helping these children succeed. She was a dream come true for us. I'd talked to her several times over the months in early spring. She'd told me to contact her again closer to the end of the school year so we could make arrangements for Jaimie. By then, I'd be in a better position to give her an update on how Jaimie did at preschool so she'd know where to start with Jaimie in the fall.

It was a load off our minds, and at the best time too, since the next few months proved to be worrisome enough.

~~~

From early May to the beginning of June, I'd gone into false labor several times. I was in the emergency room on almost a weekly basis with pain and to make sure baby Sophie's heart wasn't being adversely affected by the stress my body was under. And, as mentioned earlier, it put Jaimie through a tremendous amount of worry. She rarely left my side. She even refused to sleep, fearing I wouldn't be there when she woke up.

Sophie wasn't due until the end of June. We just prayed I'd at least make it into June before going into full-fledged labor so she had the greatest chance for survival. On top of worrying about Jaimie, I also feared losing Sophie. How does one prepare oneself for the possibility of having to say goodbye to a little life they've felt move, seen on an ultrasound, and heard their heart beating? I was scared to bond with Sophie for that very reason. And, on top of all the worry and stress, I felt guilty.

The last time I went into the hospital, my OB/GYN decided to break my water because I wanted to leave the hospital (again!) and go home to my other children, especially Jaimie.

"You're five centimeters dilated," she said. "I'm not helping you have this baby in the parking lot! You need to be here. Let's help her come out."

So our baby Sophie was born on June 9th, 2008 with a neonatal emergency team ready to whisk her off to the NICU shortly afterwards. Jaimie waited in the waiting room with Steve and my best friend, Colleen. Just before they took Sophie to the NICU, Jaimie came in and smiled one of her rare genuine big, beautiful smiles.

We figured Jaimie took a deep shining to Sophie because she'd had struggles early in her life too. When we got to visit Sophie in the NICU a few hours later, Jaimie leaned into her bassinette and whispered, "It's okay, Sophie. I'll never be afraid to hug you. And you can hug me too whenever you want, okay? If your heart needs love to be healthy, I'll give it to you."

My gorgeous little girl who never felt safe in her own world offered to make Sophie feel safe in hers. After three excruciatingly long days with all of us at home with Sophie still in the hospital, the doctors finally released her. It was found from an echocardiogram that Sophie's heart abnormality didn't affect how her heart functioned so her doctor simply needed to monitor it to ensure it never will. We still don't know what it was and aren't sure it won't ever turn into anything serious but the entire experience taught us a valuable life lesson: To worry only about what we can do something about and to leave the rest to God...or whomever watched out for us. It also taught us to live each day to the fullest and never take anything for granted.

With that insight close to my heart, I promised to do everything I could to get Jaimie into Kindergarten with the assistance she needed to achieve success.

I had the power to do that much.

~~~

In mid-August, after I'd fully recovered from having Sophie, I re-approached the situation with getting Jaimie into Kindergarten with a fresh, positive attitude. What astounded both Steve and I was that by that time, we still hadn't heard from Community Options.

"Just how long is this waiting list that Jaimie's on?" Steve kept asking me. I had no idea but I was more than annoyed. That wasn't our only problem. Initially, the school refused Jaimie's application for Kindergarten.

"Based on Jaimie's age, she should be going into Grade One," the school secretary said. "We'll have to change her application."

I was floored. "But we chose to keep Jaimie back," I said. "She was barely able to handle the social aspect of preschool and you want me to have her skip Kindergarten and go into Grade One? That's not right."

She didn't know what to say so she left a message for the principal to phone me back. *Great*, I thought. We'll have to do the pass-the-message-to-the-next-professional-on-the-list shuffle again until someone can answer our questions. Surprisingly, the principal called me back that same afternoon but his response wasn't what I'd hoped it would have been.

"We can't register Jaimie into kindergarten because she's too old," he said sharply. "I talked to our guy at Alberta Education and it would be more beneficial to Jaimie in the long run if we registered her in Grade One, and then put her in the kindergarten class. We can get the funding for her for the services she requires that way."

Ahhh, I thought. *It all comes down to money.* You can get more money if my daughter was in a higher grade. It doesn't matter that she can't handle it; only that you get your money.

I was so angry but too speechless to argue with him. I even tried telling him what Jaimie's needs were but it didn't seem to matter. So I called in the big guns—Steve.

"That's the dumbest thing I've ever heard!" he said. "No, I'm sorry. I'm calling someone from Alberta Education in the building here, and then calling that guy back myself. There's no way my daughter is skipping Kindergarten and chance failing completely just to fit into some jerk's budget. I'll call you back later."

One of the perks of Steve's position within a government agency was that he had access to other offices in the government. Essentially Steve called the head of Alberta Education in his building who told him, "Your daughter should be fine. Generally, parents decide when they enroll their children into Kindergarten. Obviously, you can't have them enrolling at age ten or something but at five and a half, you should be fine. Call me back if there are any more problems."

With that information in our corner, Steve called the principal back who stuck with his original idea: that Jaimie was past the acceptable age of registration and had to be enrolled in Grade One.

"So, you're asking me to have my daughter skip Kindergarten, jump into Grade One when she's barely able to keep it together in preschool? My kid is a very bright girl but she cannot handle the social aspect of Grade One. You're setting her up for failure and I won't let you do that to her."

"Mr. Lepp, your daughter would be in the Kindergarten class," the principal told Steve. "But she'll be enrolled in Grade One in order to get the funding for whatever assistance she needs."

It didn't make any sense to either of us.

Fine, we thought. If you want to enroll her in Grade One to get more money, whatever, as long as our daughter was in kindergarten.

Why did we need to fight so hard just to get our child into school? Mrs. P. wasn't happy about it either. Mrs. P. called me the next day. "Jaimie is registered in Kindergarten," she said. "In this province, it's up to the parents to decide when their child will start school. I brought in someone over the head of who the principal talked to in order to clarify that fact to him. Don't worry. Jaimie is in Kindergarten and she'll be with me."

I was so relieved. *Finally*, we had someone on our side—standing beside us, making sure Jaimie got the support she needed. Mrs. P. even helped us cut through all the red tape at Community Options. After a few phone calls on her part, I was told Jaimie would have the assistance she needed! I was speechless. Mrs. P. brought us further ahead and connected us to more help than we'd ever gotten either on our own or even through CASA.

Mrs. P. said I'd have to attend a meeting with her, the vice-principal, and representatives from the place giving assistance. She told me to bring as much information as I could—not only on SPD but also all of Jaimie's assessments, diagnosis, letters, reports...anything and everything I had that gave insight on Jaimie's situation. "Bring Jaimie too," she said. "That way, she'll remember our faces when she starts next week."

On the day of the meeting, a few days later, I stuffed copies of letters, reports, assessments, copies of Donna's therapy notes and her final report, letters from CASA (specifically the one the psychiatrist had written), and information on SPD into a big file folder. Heck, I even brought along my worn and ragged copy of *The Out Of Sync Child* and the children's picture book I wrote and extra sources!

As Jaimie and I walked across the field to the school, I tried easing Jaimie's mind about going to Kindergarten. "This is the way we'll come to school every day, Jaimie—except that we'll have Jordy, Xander, and Sophie with us too. And on Tuesdays and Thursdays, Jordy will be right here in the school with you."

Jaimie didn't say a word the entire walk. But she reached up and grabbed my hand. I squeezed it as we opened the doors to the school. Mrs. P. was there waiting for us.

"Mrs. Lepp? I'm Kathy," she said, sticking her hand out t
I put my hand in hers but mine was ice-cold. She knew why too.
"Oh my goodness, love. Don't worry. Everything will be fine."
She bent down to Jaimie and said, "Why don't you grab your
Mommy's hand and come with me, Jaimie."

Mrs. P. took us into the vice-principal's office where I met, and
gave icy-handshakes to, the vice-principal and the representatives
from the community assistance place. Even though I was nervous,
it was different from every other meeting I'd had in the past. I
wasn't asked millions of questions—they already seemed to
understand everything. In fact, as soon as I said Jaimie had SPD,
the head of assistance program said, "Ah...so we'll need to get
her things like some sensory seats or one of those big eggs from
IKEA. I'm assuming Jaimie can be both avoidant as well as
seeking, correct?"

My mouth dropped and I nodded.

He waved his hand at me and smiled. "Mrs. Lepp I have a lot
of experience with sensory sensitive children and children with
SPD. Don't worry. We'll get what Jaimie needs. Why don't you
give me some of Jaimie's case history so I can be sure to be in
close tuned with those needs."

I handed him my file and he took what he needed. "I see she
hasn't been in actual therapy for awhile, right?"

"We had to stop her sessions with Donna because something
about Donna bothered Jaimie so much that she wasn't able to
concentrate on her therapy. Then we were taking play therapy
through CASA but Jaimie wasn't getting what she needed from
the program anymore. Now...it's just me."

He nodded. "I know Donna well, actually. She's top notch.
And I'm in close contact with the head psychiatrist and other
therapists from there too. I can get any additional information I
need from her. This is perfect."

Jaimie wasn't able to sit still so Mrs. P. asked her if she wanted
to go get a few books and bring them back. Jaimie looked at me

with a wrinkled brow "It's okay, honey," I said. "I'll be here when you get back. Go ahead!"

After Jaimie left the room, the assistance reps and I discussed more specific details of Jaimie's needs: her triggers, her reactions to things, her need for routine...everything. They actually understood everything I was talking about. They explained they'd have to do periodic assessments on Jaimie to be sure she continued getting the resources she needed and that the funding was still provided. "Nothing will be done without your permission and you can be there for the assessments, if you'd like to." they said.

Jaimie bounded back into the room with an armful of books. Mrs. P. gave me a "thumbs up" sign. I eased. After a few more minutes of light conversation, so that Jaimie could read her books, we went home. And, for the first time since Jaimie was born, I felt an overwhelming sense of hope.

During that meeting, I was listened to and respected—which was both surprising and a relief. The funding manager had even heard of SPD and knew what Jaimie's needs were without my even having to clarify anything. I began to cry from the over-whelming feeling that finally... finally someone cared enough to listen and follow through. For the first time since Jaimie was born, I felt we were in the right place and in the right hands. Obviously, Steve and I had to continue advocating for our daughter so she didn't get forgotten about but we felt we were on the right path.

Mrs. P. is the sort of teacher who focused on a child's strengths and didn't let him or her use their special needs as excuses not to do things. She gave them options, made them feel good about their choices, and built up their confidence so they could feel good about independence. She and I set up bi-weekly meetings in order to keep a strong connection between school and home, and to maintain consistency. That's so important to Jaimie's success. And if Jaimie felt a connection between her safe place and her learning place, she'd feel good about going. That's what we wanted.

I was worried on Jaimie's first day because she broke down and was so frightened—it was like Fun Factory all over again. But Mrs. P. guided Jaimie into classroom to choose her activities. Jaimie still struggled with a high amount of anxiety so Mrs. P. always warned her and me several days in advance for sensory stimulating activities they did, walked Jaimie through everything step-by-step, and taught Jaimie how to "use her words."

Mrs. P. seemed to "get" why school may seem so stressful to Jaimie most days when it was no big deal for other children. And she shared the philosophy of Carol Stock Kranowitz of why children like Jaimie would find school more difficult than others do:

- School pressures children to perform and conform to the norm. Most children will do what he or she can to meet those expectations where children with SPD will meltdown.

- School environments have transitions that are fast-paced. Children are expected to move from math to reading to another activity with no break in between. Children like Jaimie struggle with these transitions because they need more time to adjust.

- There are a lot of sensory stimuli at school. Other kids sitting close, flickering lights, echoing sounds, different smells—these can all overwhelm a child with SPD, who will overload and meltdown.

- For other children with SPD, sitting for long periods of time with no way to release pent up energy can be excruciating. When I picked Jaimie up from Kindergarten, she couldn't get out of the building soon enough. She ran to the field between our townhouses and the school did somersaults, spun in circles, and sprinted around. In the winter, she needed to throw herself into the deep snow.

- The way lessons are presented may not be suitable to a child with SPD. Jaimie, for example, needs to see things to get them and/or feel them if she's in that mood. In a classroom, lessons that are verbal only and with no visual aides were difficult for her.

- Teachers, educational administrators, and other people often misunderstand children who display SPD symptoms. They seem to want to help but aren't always able to—or want to—accommodate their special learning needs.

- School is very different from home. School is unpredictable where life at home is safe. The child will seem different in each of these environments because what's in those environments differs. But school can become a safer place when teachers and parents work together to focus on tactics and methods that work.

There were days—and still are—where Jaimie was unable to handle the extreme sensory stimulation at school. And we had a few incidents where I had to go to the school and bring her back home because Mrs. P. wasn't able to bring her back down. But we always tried working with her at school first. When she didn't get enough sleep, or was stressed out even before leaving the house, the day ahead of her was still a challenge—for all of us.

To this day, she shies away from playing with other children, and still depends on me for a lot of things, but she's trying her best. We're all working as a team—parents, family, friends, teachers, and community assistance—to help give Jaimie the support she needs. And we've had small hints that our efforts are making a difference.

When I picked Jaimie up from school the other morning, she wasn't at the doorway itching to leave. When I peeked in the door, I saw her standing beside a little girl who was seated at the writing table. Just as I was about to call her over to leave, Jaimie bent down to the little girl, allowing her to touch her hat, coat, and ski pants. I watched in awe as Jaimie then allowed the little girl to touch her face and hands.

"Good bye, Jaimie," the little girl said. "I really like your hat and other winter stuff!"

"Bye-bye, Rita," Jaimie answered with a huge smile we rarely see. "I'll bring my Care Bear tomorrow."

Mrs. A., the Aide, approached me to explain the miraculous scene. "Jaimie and Rita have developed quite a strong bond. Rita is blind and since her first day, she and Jaimie seemed drawn to one another. Rita 'sees' by touch so we were worried at first how Jaimie would react. We always ask Jaimie whether it's okay with her to be touched. You should see… Rita puts her hands all over Jaimie's arms, face, hands, hair, and clothes—just like a few minutes ago—and Jaimie never minds. It has Kathy and me crying each time."

Jaimie teaches Rita different ways to 'see' things, and Rita teaches Jaimie that touch isn't always terrifying. Kids amaze me. God has certainly brought certain people in our lives for specific reasons…sometimes just in the nick of time.

We finally have all of the support we'll need to make sure she'll continue making her mark in this world. From now on, Jaimie's voice will be heard and I'll do everything in my power to make it be heard.

Jaimie will always have SPD but she learned—and continues to learn—how to cope with it. She showed us all that even with a broken wing, any of us can still fly if other people just take the time to listen and try to understand without judging.

All your life, you were only waiting for this moment to be free.

12 | Blackbird Fly: Endnotes for Parents

When I was growing up, "Blackbird" (1968) by The Beatles was one of my mother's favorite songs. John Lennon always said people could take what they needed to from his lyrics and, for the people in my life. The words in that particular song have always been a source of comfort. When I became a Mom, it was the song I sang to Jaimie to help calm her down enough to focus on my words. To me, I always felt as if John was trying to say that we all have things about us that are different and once we accept those differences, we can help make other people accept them as well.

One thing I've learned through all of our struggles with Jaimie was that we reach a level of understanding by being willing to put aside what we see or what we think we know. If Jaimie was taking lessons on how to interact with other people, then I had to help other people learn how to interact with her too. Otherwise there was no point in giving Jaimie her coping tools.

There were just a few important things I thought parents should know. First, Jaimie's form of SPD is quite severe. I certainly don't want to generalize our case to *all* cases of SPD. Some children only deal with certain sensory struggles, some are only dealing with gross and/or fine motor skills and others, like Jaimie, struggle in all areas. The best thing to do is to watch, look and listen: *Watch* how a child interacts with his or her environment and the people in it; *Look* what they are trying to tell you and how they are trying to communicate; and *Listen* both to your child and to your gut.

Donna Gravelle, the wonderful OT who first worked with Jaimie, told me to trust my gut and that, in her experience, when parents feel in their gut—their very soul—that there's a problem, there usually is. That's not to say there aren't children out there who are "just spirited" or whose emotions are right at the surface all of the time. But there's a very fine line between a child who is spirited and one who has more serious issues.

A child who is spirited may run around at full kilt, is very active, and doesn't like to settle down. He or she may even be choosy about certain activities or events. But these things may not prevent them from living their lives and enjoying being a kid. Alternatively, a child whose choosiness or "spirited nature" affects his or her everyday life, how he or she interacts with the environment or the people in it, or impedes their enjoyment of life, may have a more serious issue that requires closer attention.

The other point I wanted to help parents with is trying not to fear therapy. Allow me to explain. I won't lie—I was incredibly nervous about putting Jaimie into therapy. She wasn't able to function with us at the best of times; then, suddenly, different people showed up at our home—or we took her out to people— wanting to work closely with her, getting her trying the very things that terrified her. I hated seeing her screaming, struggling, and fighting with those people, and it took every ounce of strength not to run to her and intervene. But, as I realized later on, these activities were exactly what Jaimie needed.

All of Jaimie's life, up to the point when Donna entered our lives, we helped her avoid any activities, people, places or other things that caused her distress. I didn't realize that I added to the problem. If Jaimie wasn't allowed to experience any of the sensory things around her, how was she ever going to learn how to function in her world? I wouldn't have been able to live with myself knowing that I contributed to her distress rather than helped her with it.

Bearing that in mind helped me get through watching as she screamed, cried, and fought as people tried tuning her into the world around her. And what also helped me grin and bear it was conducting research on the various therapies and the people who'd worked with her, the tactics they'd most likely have tried, and why they needed to do it. It eased my mind to understand.

Just as Donna explained to us during her first few visits (as I stood in the background, biting my nails and holding back tears), "Jaimie's brain doesn't understand how to process these stimulations. So we need to jolt her brain to the stimulation but do it in fun ways so she'll learn to relate the stimulation to fun instead of fear."

Steve and I wrote our feelings down and read them over every time we felt like pulling Jaimie out of therapy due to her reactions. We called it, "Our Oath to Jaimie's Advocacy." It was our way of reminding ourselves, "Yes, we are doing the right thing... we hope..."

Keeping these things in mind calmed our nerves during Jaimie's first assessment and kept us focused through the rest of our therapy journey:

Take what you find helpful and put rest aside: This doesn't mean forget about what you're told—just to put it away in case you need it later. Parents get a lot of information, advice, and suggestions about what they should do. It can be intimidating and, at times, parents may feel pressured to do what they're told is best. After all, these are the experts, right? *Yes and no.*

Yes, they are the experts in their fields but parents are the experts with their child and only they know what's best. Parents should never feel bullied or pressured to do anything they don't think will be good for their child nor will help them. And, as we found out, parents should always be sure to voice their opinions and what they want for their child.

For example, there were two things Steve and I wouldn't back down on with Jaimie: (a) we wanted to find an effective non-medicinal way to help her learn to cope with her SID; and (b) the therapist would do best with Jaimie by working within her routine and gradually expanding on it. As soon as Jaimie feels uncomfortable or scared, she introverts and we can't get her back out. This means starting back at square one (something we, and the first OT who worked with Jaimie, figured out the hard way.)

Parents need to filter through all of that information to find what they think will work best, do the research, and then get everyone on the same page. In the end, that's what everyone involved wants: what's best for the child. And the final stamp on what's best is up to the parent.

Ask a lot of questions: Parents should never be afraid to ask questions whether about what's involved with a specific treatment, something they've researched and want more information on, or even more information about the expert's credentials. A parent probably needs to deal with those experts for a long time so they may as well get any uncertainties out in the open. A true professional won't mind any questions and respect the desire to be as informed as possible.

Consult with someone who's been there: When Jaimie was finally next on the infamous waiting list for the program we wanted to get her into, I met with the Head of the Edmonton Early Intervention program, Joan MacDonald. She was an invaluable source for me because she had a teenage daughter with SPD. As soon as she met Jaimie, she said her daughter was exactly like her as a toddler.

Talking with someone who's been there serves several purposes. First, parents get the heads up about what the assessments will be like. It helps ease the mind a bit to have some insight ahead of time. Second, and what I found most helpful, is that a person who's been there can show how things can get better and give a look into what the future holds. Finally, it just feels good to talk with someone who's been there, and continues to be. It's wonderful to have supportive friends and family around offering words of encouragement and love, bless their hearts. But, truly, the only people who understand the frustration, the heartache, the worry are other parents of a child with SPD.

The most important thing to keep in mind, which I have a tendency to forget myself sometimes, is that all of the experts are there to help us parent Jaimie most effectively and help her learn the skills she needs to enjoy her childhood to the fullest.

Be strong, be patient, and never be afraid to address questions or concerns.

~~~

Penny Lee Kelly wrote a phenomenal synopsis regarding her daughter, Katie. She too wanted to bring understanding for her daughter and awareness for SPD. It was her powerful words that inspired me to write about Jaimie:

"There has been so much advice given in all the books I have read on SI Dysfunction. I think the most important advice was the following insights: to pay attention to your child (remember that your child's problem is a physical one and the indigestion of the brain causes her behavior – she can't help acting the way she is acting); know your child's strengths and weaknesses (get as much information as you can); anticipate responses (develop strategies to cope with negative emotions before they occur); empathize (understand the child's feelings and reflect them back); provide structure (establish routines and schedules); be consistent with discipline; and become your child's advocate.

I think that last piece of advice is why I wrote this synopsis for Katie. I need to educate adults who need to know about Katie's abilities. SI Dysfunction is invisible and people tend to forget or disbelieve that a significant problem affects my child. My job as her parent is to inform you so you can help my child learn and develop to her fullest potential."

I want people to look at Jaimie and see a smiling, beautiful little girl. I want to bring about understanding to her and children like her. There are many folks out there who don't even believe SPD is an actual disorder. They erroneously believe all these children need is, perhaps, a stronger hand of discipline.

Like Penny Lee, Steve and I struggled for several years before Jaimie's diagnosis for empathy and understanding. Even now, if Jaimie isn't able to hold it together well, we'll have people suggest, "Give her a good spanking. That's all she needs!" or "It's just a behavioral problem." We don't get angry or defensive anymore because, honestly, people simply don't understand that Jaimie struggles every single day with things we can't even see.

People don't understand that it may have been their perfume, breath, or house smells on their clothes that set Jaimie off. They don't understand that standing too close to her or touching her in any way drives her crazy. And they don't get that on top of those smells or the fear of being touched or the way their faces move when they talk or that one flickering light of in the distance, she's scared to lose it because then…then people will know something is wrong with her and she'll feel even worse.

Jaimie is a very intelligent girl. In fact, she's developmentally ahead of most kids her age. She's creative, funny, loving, and warm. But her body won't let her feel safe enough to let too many people see those beautiful traits in her. For Jaimie, it's better to avoid the activities or people that make her insides go crazy— even when she sees such things are fun for others—than to risk being over-stimulated and not be able to calm herself down. It's terrifying for her and it's what she'd been trying to tell us all those years before she could talk.

What I want most in the world for these children is understanding. It starts with parents and guardians. We need to create a strong support group, get our child's physicians on our side in order to access the community assistance and to arm ourselves with as much knowledge as we can. Knowledge is very powerful and it's also contagious. Maybe if we all tell our stories, if we all reach out together, it'll happen.

On my most frustrating days, I simply look down on Jaimie's earnest little face and think, "My God. How strong and courageous she is just to get out of bed in the morning and face what her environment has in store for her. If she can do it, so can I!"

Jaimie is six now. It was difficult for her to concentrate on her learning at first. And we had several days where her teachers and Aide weren't able to calm her, resulting in me having to come get her. But despite all of that, Mrs. P, the Aid and I worked together helping Jaimie face every challenge with the proper tools:

- We were sure never to make her feel singled out for anything. When we had to incorporate one of Jaimie's sensory tools into her school plan, such as her squeezable ball to help with paying attention and/or working through an anxious situation, it was made to be no big deal and just one of her learning supplies.

- The IKEA egg she was supplied with was utilized by all of her classmates whenever any of them needed a "calm time." Mrs. P. made sure to explain that the egg was a "calming chair" not a "time-out chair," which was kept in an entirely different part of the classroom. That way Jaimie never associated it with being bad.

- Mrs. P. had a few other children who'd had writing difficulties so she bought a big supply of pencil grippers of different colors and designs. This made Jaimie so happy since she had some fine motor skill struggles too.

- Jaimie's Aide came up with a wonderful book she made for Jaimie called, "Jaimie's Book" where Jaimie got to work through potentially stressful situations by writing and reading. The word "plan" worked really well with Jaimie. It seemed to calm her because she actually had to brainstorm about solutions to her problems. Then she and her Aide wrote a story about how Jaimie was faced with _____ (whatever the problem was) but Jaimie would be okay because she could _____ (the solutions Jaimie came up with.) It was brilliant and we do that here at home now too.

- Worked with Jaimie all year long on how to use her words instead of acting out or shutting down. Jaimie will still need help with this but the seed was planted.

- Allowed Jaimie to watch other kids doing activities that were uncomfortable before her so she could decide if she wanted to give it a try or, if she wasn't able to handle the activity on that day, got her to come up with another way she could participate. For example, if they worked with wet clay, which Jaimie wasn't always able to handle, she chose to do the craft wearing gloves and they made sure to have a bucket of water and a cloth right beside the work table so that she could wash her hands.

- Near the end of the year, we had Jaimie attend school all day in order to prepare her for the Grade One setting. We were also able to meet with the teacher, which really helped Jaimie.

These were just a few of the wonderful things they did. They also listened to me when I requested that Jaimie have more physical activity during her day because it calmed her and she didn't seem as klutzy later on. Mrs. P. took them outside when it was nice; let them run around and play in the gym when it was rainy or too cold; and gave Jaimie "special jobs" to do—like taking things to the principal or walking with her blind friend, Rita. The most important thing to help our SPD children in public school is to communicate with the teachers and other educators on a daily basis. They can't help our children in school if we don't share what will help from our perspective and we can't help our children at home if we don't know what bumps they encountered during their school day.

Finally, Jaimie's sensitivity to certain textures is still rather high but she's at least becoming braver in trying certain foods. We now have a "one bite rule" in the house for everyone. We also have two options in line for when Jaimie's eating more of a variety of foods:

- We discovered the Feingold Program (www. feingold.org), which isn't a diet but what they call an "elimination and replacement" process. Basically we take everything out of our diets that have artificial flavors, coloring, or dyes. It's an awesome program because you aren't really giving up anything; you're simply making better choices. And with all of the research showing how additives in our foods affect even the healthiest individuals, we love the philosophy behind this program.

- We plan to incorporate certain gluten-free/casein-free recipes and meals into our diet. Children with certain behavioral problems or neurological disorders, such as autism and SPD, have shown a great reduction in symptoms after removing gluten and casein from their diets. We won't know for sure if that's how it is for Jaimie but it's an option for down the road.

Jaimie graduated from kindergarten in June 2009—we couldn't be more proud of her. We had to fight to get her into a regular class as well as for the help she'll need to cope with school, but we did it. People are finally listening to us. In fact, the teacher she has for Grade One is not only interested in learning everything she can about SPD so that she can help Jaimie through the next school year, she also shared a story with me about how she recognized the symptoms in a child she'd had in her class the year before. She helped to guide the parents to the treatment that child needed to thrive. I don't think I have to tell you the relief we feel.

Today, Jaimie still has bad days and struggles with every day activities. But she's doing her best and that's all that matters. The fact that my little girl who feared leaving the house actually performed in a Christmas concert and went ice skating shows her Dad and I that everything we're doing for her, and continue to do for her, makes a difference.

Don't give up! Things will be okay.

The Key to Serenity

Acceptance is the answer to all my problems today. When I am disturbed, it is because I find some person, place, thing, or situation--Some fact of my life--unacceptable to me, and I can find no serenity until I accept that person, place, thing, or situation as being exactly the way it is supposed to be at this moment. Nothing, absolutely nothing happens in God's world by mistake. Unless I accept life completely on life's terms, I cannot be happy. I need to concentrate not so much on what needs to be changed in the world as on what needs to be changed in me and in my attitudes.

Alcoholics Anonymous Big Book, 4th Ed.

About the Author: Chynna T. Laird

Where did you grow up?

I grew up in Winnipeg, Manitoba in Canada with my younger brother, Cam. We actually moved around a lot but always stayed in Winnipeg.

Why you are uniquely qualified to write this book?

My daughter, Jaimie, was diagnosed with Sensory Processing Disorder (SPD) when she was 2-½. I'm not an expert or a therapist—I'm just a mom who struggled to find someone to help me understand my child so I could help her.

Why did you write this book?

We'd struggled for over two years prior to Jaimie's diagnosis not only with figuring out how to help Jaimie but simply trying to get someone just to listen to our concerns. I did a lot of research, interviewed many people—including experts in the SPD and autism communities—and wrote a lot during our journey. Once we were on the right path, I decided to use the information and knowledge I gained to help other parents who were in the same situation we were in.

There weren't as many resources when we began our journey, especially for those here in Canada. I wanted to contribute a project that wasn't just explaining what SPD is or how to detect it but more to give parents some comfort that they aren't "the only ones" going through this and, maybe, inspire them to keep on going—keep fighting, keep knocking on doors and to never give up.

What do you think readers will get out of it?

The main message I'm hoping readers will get from our story is "look beyond the surface." If I've learned nothing else in life it's that an overt behavior is never the only indication that something is wrong—it's most often a symptom. Parents should always listen to that gut feeling—that intuition in the pit of the stomach telling us that something is amiss—and search for answers until you're exhausted then keep right on searching until you find the *right* answers, the *right*, diagnosis and the *right* way to help your child. Only *you* know what would work.

What will you do next in your life?

I have a reference book about the Sensory Diet coming out in January 2011. I'll also continue to write, research, and speak on raising a child with SPD. I also have a couple of fiction projects in the works as well as another memoir on living with a mother who had untreated bipolar disorder and alcoholism. The memoir about my mom is a story to help those understand the importance of diagnosis and treatment for mental illness. There's such a stigma placed on these people and that's often why they won't seek the help they desperately need. I'm hoping my story will show why treatment is so important for a sufferer's entire family, especially when they have children.

~~~

You can get in touch with Chynna and find out about all her latest projects at **www.lilywolfwords.ca**

Resources and Websites

- **Lily Wolf Words** (my personal website packed full with stories, links to helpful resources, book and product recommendations and a newsletter) please visit **www.lilywolfwords.ca**
- **SPD Foundation:** www.spdfoundation.net
- **Sensory Processing Disorder Resource Center:** www.sensory-processing-disorder.com
- **Sensory Critters.com:** www.sensorycritters.com
- **Kid Power site** www.kid-power.org/sid.html
- **Sensory Integration Dysfunction:** http://home.comcast.net/~momtofive/SIDWEBPAGE2.htm
- **One Mom's Synopsis on the subject of SID/SPD:** http://www.kid-power.org/sid/sidsynopsis.html
- **SPD Canada:** www.spdcanada.org
- **Sensory Fun** (Bonnie Arnwine): www.sensoryfun.com
- **Sensory Resources:** www.sensoryresources.com
- **Sensory Smarts:** www.sensorysmarts.com
- **Sensory Street:** www.sensorystreet.com
- **S.I. Focus magazine site:** www.sifocus.com

There are also fantastic online parent support groups on YahooGroups.com. Search for SPD groups on the YahooGroups page and choose what works best for you.

Bibliography

Arnwine, B., & McCoy, O. (2007). *Starting sensory integration therapy: Fun activities that won't destroy your home or classroom!* Arlington, Tex: Future Horizons.

Auer, C. R., & Blumberg, S. L. (2006). *Parenting a child with sensory processing disorder: A family guide to understanding and supporting your sensory-sensitive child.* Oakland, CA: New Harbinger Publications.

Ayres, A. J., Erwin, P. R., & Mailloux, Z. (2004). *Love, Jean: Inspiration for families living with dysfunction of sensory integration.* Santa Rosa, CA: Crestport Press

Biel, L., & Peske, N. K. (2005). *Raising a sensory smart child: The definitive handbook for helping your child with sensory integration issues.* New York: Penguin Books.

Canfield, J. (2008). *Chicken soup for the soul: Children with special needs.* Deerfield Beach, Fla: Health Communications.

Kranowitz, C. S. (2005). *The out-of-sync child: Recognizing and coping with sensory processing disorder.* New York: A Skylight Press Book/A Perigee Book.

Kranowitz, C. S., & Wylie, T. J. (2004). *The Goodenoughs get in sync: A story for kids about the tough day when Filibuster grabbed Darwin's rabbit foot...: an introduction for sensory processing disorder and sensory integration.* Las Vegas: Sensory Resources.

Laird, D. *I'm not weird, i have sid.* (2007) Outskirts Press.

Miller, L. J., & Fuller, D. A. (2006). *Sensational kids: Hope and help for children with sensory processing disorder (SPD)*. New York: G.P. Putnam's Sons.

Renna, D. M., Stark, R., & Renna, M. (2007). *Meghan's world: The story of one girl's triumph over sensory processing disorder*. Speonk, NY: Indigo Impressions.

Szklut, S., Kranowitz, C. S., & Koomar, J. (2007). *Answers to questions teachers ask about sensory integration (including sensory processing disorder)*. Arlington, Texas: Future Horizons.

Books on Anxiety, OCD, and Worrying

The following books I've added to my personal library because they are wonderful in teaching children how to deal with, cope with, and connect to his or her feelings. We've found all of them tremendously useful, especially the ones where kids get to write and draw too.

Bloomquist, M. L., & Bloomquist, M. L. (2006). *Skills training for children with behavior problems: A parent and practitioner guidebook*. New York: Guilford Press.

Buron, K. D. (2006). *When my worries get too big!: A relaxation book for children who live with anxiety*. Shawnee Mission, Kan: Autism Asperger Pub.

Fitzgibbons, L., & Pedrick, C. (2003). *Helping your child with OCD: A workbook for parents of children with obsessive-compulsive disorder*. Oakland, CA: New Harbinger Publications.

Huebner, D., & Matthews, B. (2006). *What to do when you worry too much: A kid's guide to overcoming anxiety. "What to do" guides for kid*s. Washington, D.C.: Magination Press.

Jaffe, A. V., & Gardner, L. (2005). *My book full of feelings: How to control and react to the size of your emotions.* Shawnee Mission, Kan: Autism Asperger Pub.

Stallard, P. (2002). *Think good, feel good: A CBT workbook for young people.* New York: Wiley.

Index

A

antioxidants, 92
anxiety, 78, 90, 144
Asperger's, xi, 35, 36, 37
autism, xi, 8, 34, 35, 36, 43, 97, 135
   vs. SPD, 43
autonomic nervous system, 92
Axline, V., 79
Ayres, A.J., xi, xii

C

chiropractic, 101
choline, 93
communication skills, 8, 44
Community Options, 89, 90, 115, 118,
   120
coping skills, vii, 65
craniosacral therapy, 101

D

dancing, 18
diapers, 29, 31, 38
diet, 91–94
   sensory, 100
discipline, 51, 65, 96, 131, 132
dressing, 16

E

Early Intervention Program. *See* EIP
eating, 12, 13–14
Edmonton, 12, 41, 63, 98, 130

EIP, vi, 41, 69, 74
eliminating, 14
eye contact, 16, 32, 36, 53, 78, 107

F

Feingold Program, 135

G

Gravelle, D., 42, 128
group therapy, 97

H

head banging, vi, 6, 17, 26, 40, 41, 56,
   See also self-harm
home visits, 97
hospital preschool intervention, 98

I

IKEA egg, 133

K

Kelly, P., 131, 132
Kranowitz, C., vii, 44, 99, 100, 101, 123,
   143

M

MacDonald, J., 130
magnesium, 92
Miller, L., xii
moving house, 33

N

NICU, 114, 117
night terrors, 6, 12, 82
nonverbal communication, 8

O

Obsessive-Compulsive Disorder. *See* OCD
occupational therapist, vi, 21, 64, 71, 97
OCD, 78, 144
Omega-3, 91, 92, 93
over-responsive, vii, viii

P

perceptual motor therapy, 102
physical therapy, 101
Pinel, J., xi
Play Therapy, 78, 79, 82, 96, 98
   preparation, 80
preschool, 44, 63, 75, 80, 87, 89, 95, 97,
   102, 106–11, 113, 115, 116, 118, 119
proprioceptive, ix–x
psychiatrist, 63, 64, 71, 75, 77, 84, 85,
   86, 87, 89, 91, 120, 121
psychologist, 6, 71, 74, 97

R

repetitive behaviors, 8, 35
routine
   need for, 34, 35

S

school, 123–25
self-harm, 17
sensory overload, ix, xii, 36

sensory questionnaire, 50
sleeping, 15
social interaction, 8, 36, 85
socializing, 16
SPD
   and SID, xii
   assessment, vii
   causes, x
   defined, vii–viii
   diagnosis, vii
   in adults, xi
   resources, 141
speech therapist, 64, 66, 98, 99, 101

T

tactile, viii–ix
Tilton, A., 36
toilet training, 14, 38
triggers, 8, 103
tyrosine, 92

U

Upledger
   J., 101

V

vestibular, ix
vitamins, 91, 92, 93, 99

W

worrying, 144

Y

YMCA, 102, 106, 107, 111

What if we could resolve childhood trauma early, rather than late?

We are understanding more and more about how early traumatic experiences affect long-term mental and physical health:

• Physical impacts are stored in muscles and posture

• Threats of harm are stored as tension

• Overwhelming emotion is held inside

• Negative emotional patterns become habit

• Coping and defense mechanism become inflexible

What if we could resolve childhood trauma before years go by and these effects solidify in body and mind?

In a perfect world, we'd like to be able to shield children from hurt and harm. In the real world, children, even relatively fortunate ones, may experience accidents, injury, illness, and loss of loved ones. Children unfortunate enough to live in unsafe environments live through abuse, neglect, and threats to their well-being and even their life.

Children and Traumatic Incident Reduction: Creative and Cognitive Approaches

Edited by Marian K. Volkman, CTS, CMF

Experts Praise *Children and Traumatic Incident Reduction*

"This book is a must for any therapist working with kids. Naturally, it focuses on the approach of Traumatic Incident Reduction, but there is a lot of excellent material that will be useful even to the therapist who has never before heard of TIR and may not be particularly interested in learning about it. The general approach is respectful of clients, based on a great deal of personal experience by contributors as well as on the now extensive research base supporting TIR, and fits the more general research evidence on what works".

—Robert Rich, PhD

"Much useful and thoroughly researched information is packed into this priceless volume in the TIR Application Series. This is a good book for parents to read because s/he may take away an understanding of the many different therapy strategies available to them and their children."

—Lisa Bullert, *Reader Views*

ISBN 978-1-932690-30-9   **List $19.95**

More information at www.TIRbook.com

CPSIA information can be obtained at www.ICGtesting.com
Printed in the USA
BVOW001703100713

325562BV00003B/127/P

9 781615 990085